HUNTERS
OF THE WHALE

AN ADVENTURE
IN NORTHWEST COAST
ARCHAEOLOGY
BY RUTH KIRK
WITH RICHARD D. DAUGHERTY

Hunters
of the Whale

PHOTOGRAPHS BY RUTH AND LOUIS KIRK
WILLIAM MORROW AND COMPANY
NEW YORK 1974

3   4   5

Library of Congress Cataloging in Publication Data

Kirk, Ruth.
  Hunters of the whale.

  SUMMARY: Describes an archaeological dig at Ozette, Washington, on the site of a Makah Indian village inhabited for at least 2,000 years.
  1. Ozette Indian Village—Juvenile literature. [1. Makah Indians. 2. Ozette Indian Village. 3. Indians of North America] I. Daugherty, Richard D., (date) II. Kirk, Louis, illus. III. Title.
E99.M19K57 1974   970.3   73-17317
ISBN 0-688-20109-1
ISBN 0-688-30109-6 (lib. bdg.)

Maps and diagram by Madge Gleeson

Bird and wolf motifs on binding adapted by Dale Croes from original carvings found in the Ozette house

Photographs by Ruth and Louis Kirk except as follows: Asahel Curtis Collection, Washington State Historical Society, 17, 49; Gerald Grosso, Ozette Project, 118-119, 130; Ozette Project, 71; Don Paxon, *Port Angeles Evening News,* 82; Harvey S. Rice, Washington State University, 100, 102; Roy Scully, *Seattle Times,* 118, top.

To Congresswoman Julia Butler Hansen
for her long-standing interest
in the history of her home state
and her active support
of the Ozette excavations.

CONTENTS

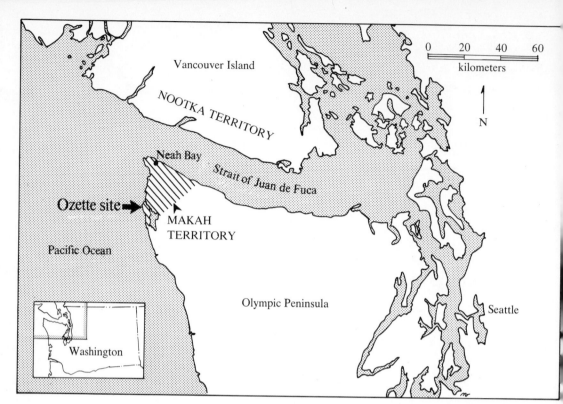

Above: Map showing location of Ozette site.

Right: Plan view of house excavation area.

Below: Map of Ozette site.

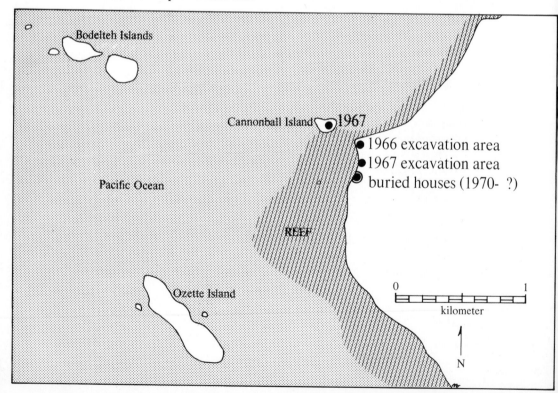

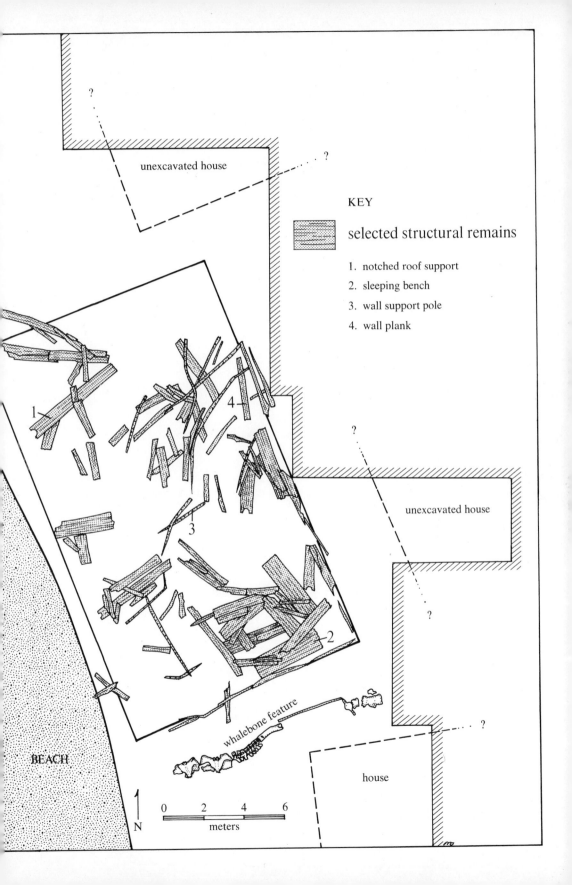

?

unexcavated house

?

KEY

selected structural remains

1. notched roof support
2. sleeping bench
3. wall support pole
4. wall plank

4

1

?

3

unexcavated house

?

2

?

whalebone feature

BEACH

house

0   2   4   6

meters

N

FOREWORD

We Makahs look in a special way at what is coming from the mud at Ozette, for this is our heritage. Now we can see what life used to be like and add this to what we remember and what our elders have told us. We can hold the household equipment and the hunting and fishing gear that our ancestors designed and made and used. The carving on the boxes and bowls and hunting clubs shows that our people have always valued beauty. The harpoons of yew wood with mussel-shell blades and elk-bone barbs used for taking whales show the strength and skill and bravery of the people.

Our ancestors lived richly by utilizing the raw materials of the forest and the sea. A few of us can remember the very last of those old days. All of us have heard our parents and grandparents tell about them. Now our young people can see for themselves, and so can all the nation. Ozette is like opening the door of a museum—for us, a museum of our own past.

Makah Tribal Council. Joseph Lawrence, chairman, at right.

There is another way that this archaeological project has been ours too. We have helped. Makah students have joined with Washington State University students, working with them at the excavations. We also have helped in the laboratory with the cleaning and cataloging of the thousands of items from the old house and, once in a while, helping to identify something that we remember from childhood, but that the archaeologists cannot recognize.

We plan to build a special museum for all of the Ozette material. There are about 20,000 artifacts in the laboratory now, and two or three times that many more are sure to be found as the excavations continue. The museum will be built by Makahs and staffed by Makahs who have been trained by the University of Washington Burke Museum and the Smithsonian Institution. It will let us share our cultural past with the nation and in that way contribute to the understanding so much needed these days. It is time that peoples with different backgrounds and ideas should see into each others' lives. There is just one earth, and we are all on it together.

We appreciate the way Dr. Richard Daugherty and his crew have gone about the work at Ozette, and we are glad to have this book as a record.

The Makah Tribal Council
Neah Bay, Washington
Autumn, 1973

I
SCIENTIFIC
DETECTIVE WORK

Rain dripped from the spruce trees and a seal stuck its head out of the water where waves were swelling and beginning their slow roll toward the beach. Dr. Richard Daugherty, an archaeologist, lifted a heavy whale jawbone from the deposits on the Washington coast where he was digging. It lay a meter below the surface, crumbly and gray with age.

Whale hunters must have camped here.

Daugherty scraped deeper. His trowel flicked aside bits of white clamshell and blue mussel shell, and sharp pieces of rock that had cracked and broken in the heat of ancient cooking fires. Nothing special. Then his eyes lit on a small piece of bone. It was smooth and pointed, only about ten centi-

Left: Dr. Richard Daugherty
examined barbs from a whale harpoon.

meters long and as thick as a man's thumb. A second piece lay close by. These were barbs from a harpoon, and Daugherty realized what they meant.

Long ago eight men must have paddled a canoe close to a whale as it came up to breathe. The captain sat in the stern studying the whale as it repeatedly dove and surfaced. He watched the huge dark shadow underwater and followed it. When the time was right to paddle, the captain told the crew. He told them when they should stay quiet too. One wrong order and none of the men would go whaling again; a slap of the whale's tail could break the canoe.

At last the moment came. The whale surfaced, and the canoe rode in the water almost on top of it, slightly to the left and behind so as to be out of the whale's vision. The harpooner stood and raised his long, heavy weapon. The captain watched intently. He waited until the whale was just beginning to dive and its tail was ready for a downstroke. Then he let out a sharp cry. With all possible strength the harpooner lunged toward the whale's side, aiming for a spot just behind the flipper. He thrust in the sharp mussel-shell point of his harpoon. Blood turned the water red. The harpoon held.

A photograph taken around 1900 gives a glimpse of what such hunts must have been like. It shows a harpooner standing in the bow of a canoe with his harpoon ready to strike. Whale hunting was rare anywhere in the world before the days of modern equipment, yet on the northwest tip of Washington State men dared to pit themselves against the giants of the deep. They hunted all kinds of whales—gray whales, sperm whales, sulphur-bottoms, humpbacks—enormous animals. Gray whales are almost equal in size to railroad cars—forty

Right, top: Whaling canoes could hold eight-man crews. Harpoons were heavy and as much as fifteen feet long. *Center:* A hunter stood in the bow and thrust his harpoon into a whale. *Bottom:* The men worked the whale ashore, sealskin floats still attached as support.

feet long and as heavy as twenty tons. Baby grays are twelve feet long and weigh a full ton at birth.

Life for Indian tribes along the Northwest Coast was uncommonly rich compared to that of most tribes elsewhere. Men split wide planks for houses from cedar logs and hollowed canoes as much as thirty-five feet long which were spread by steaming to a width of six feet. Trees grew so big that fifteen boys with arms outstretched could barely reach around the trunks. Deer and elk roamed the forest. Salmon swam the rivers in such numbers that the first white men to pioneer the land joked they could cross the water by stepping

Elk . . .

on the backs of the fish. Berries grew in the forest, and there were clams to dig on the beach whenever the tide was low.

Offshore, fur seals came by the thousands. Hunters could get more meat at sea than in the forest, and with canoes they could bring it right to the village doorstep. The sea animals provided oil as well as meat. They have thick layers of fatty blubber that protect them from the icy cold of ocean water, and oil cooked out of the blubber tasted good on dried fish and could be traded to tribes who had none. It was highly prized. A layer of fat helped to shield the Indians' bodies from the cold, just as it shielded the sea mammals.

salmon . . .   seal.

No man was more honored than a hunter of whales. A single success meant meat and oil for the whole village and also bone to make into tools. Along the Washington coast the Makahs and one or two tribes to the south accepted the challenge of whale hunting and found the reward worth the risk. Indians on Vancouver Island, British Columbia, also hunted whales. But there were no more whaling tribes for the whole 1,000 miles of the rest of the Canadian coast and well up into Alaska. Then, about where the land strings westward to form the Aleutian Islands and on around the Arctic coast, Eskimos and Aleuts hunted whales.

Small islands dot the wild and rugged north coast of Washington.

Why the huge gap? Why had people so widely separated developed whale hunting, whereas those in between had not? Daugherty wanted to find out, and he knew that years of excavation and study would be needed to answer the question. The harpoon barbs were one of the many clues that would be needed.

The year was 1961. Daugherty was at White Rock on the wild outer coast of the Olympic Peninsula, reached by a four-mile hike through the forest. He was digging with seven of his students from Washington State University, in Pullman. Three years earlier other students of his had dug at Toleak

Point, a few miles to the south. If only enough of the clues hidden in the earth could be found it should be possible to solve at least part of the puzzle about the whalers. Archaeologists really know very little about prehistoric Indian life along the Northwest Coast, and each day at White Rock meant accomplishing a little more of the slow detective work needed to piece together the past.

Daugherty had another reason for wondering about this coast and its people, a personal reason. This was home country. He had been born in Aberdeen, not far south of White Rock and Toleak. As a boy he could walk along the beach and feel that little had changed since the days when Indians traveled the coast in their canoes. Nobody was hunting whales anymore. The last one had been taken about 1910. But the older men still told about the hunt. Even today the Olympic coast is wild, and much of it is without roads.

Growing up in Aberdeen meant heading into the forest every afternoon when school let out. Cascara bark could be peeled from the trees and sold to wholesalers for use in making medicine—three cents a pound if you sold it wet, seven cents if you took the trouble to dry it. There were wild blackberries to pick too. Few plants have as wicked thorns, but the berries brought seventy-five cents a gallon in pocket money. In autumn migrating ducks landed on ponds close to the beach, and a shotgun and a few shells were all it took to bring home meat for the table. Cutthroat trout lurked in green pools along the rivers, and sometimes one of the Indian men had room in his dugout canoe to take a boy fishing.

In college Daugherty studied anthropology, the science of man and his various cultures. One summer he worked in

eastern Washington, Idaho, Montana, and Wyoming, check-
ing for evidence of prehistoric Indian campsites. New dams
were being built, and their reservoirs would send water flood-
ing across vast areas, covering the sites and destroying any
chance to unravel the human past. When fall came, he began
the same kind of search for signs of early Indian occupation
along the Washington coast. Brush grew jungle thick, and
since few roads eased the problem of travel, people seldom
went there or paid much attention to the entire 150 miles
from the Columbia River to Cape Flattery.

Daugherty worked alone. Sometimes he went in by boat

Daugherty hiked through an arch worn by waves.

Stone maul and fishing weight found
during the survey of the Washington coast.

when the tide was right. Other times he fought through dense
salal brush and salmonberry bushes higher than his head. He
talked to anyone who might know where indications of an
Indian camp showed along the beach, and he watched for
likely places for camps or villages to have been. Fresh water
would have been needed, and ideally there should be an easy
place to land canoes. The biggest villages seemed to have
been at river mouths, where salmon leave the ocean to begin
their spawning runs. A sure sign was "midden," the term
archaeologists use for the piles of refuse left where people
have lived. This was the sort of rubble that held the whalebones and harpoon barbs at White Rock. Anywhere there
was shell combined with charcoal, Daugherty knew that man
had been present. Sometimes he found fishhooks, or bones,
or stone knife blades lying with the shell. Baskets and paddles
and harpoon shafts couldn't be expected to have lasted because wood and other plant materials almost always rot
quickly. A total of fifty sites were located along the coast
that autumn of 1947. Daugherty recorded each one on a

special form. What did the site look like? How deep was the midden? How far into the brush did it extend? How far up and down the beach?

One site stood out above all others: Ozette. On a particularly rainy day Daugherty hiked there. Mud squished over his

The search led along the beaches and over the headlands.

ankles most of the three miles through the forest. After an hour of walking, he began to hear the sound of surf mixed with that of wind and rain, and ahead a high bank covered by waist-high sword ferns led to the beach. Daugherty climbed down, noticing midden as he went. Not just a little midden. Lots of it. The earth of the entire bank was dark with decayed organic material and heavily dotted with bits of animal bone and seashell. Indians had told of a large village just back from this beach. A few houses still were evident, although the people had moved out twenty or thirty years before.

A terrace ran for a mile along the beach, high enough to be protected from the pounding winter storm waves and broad enough for many houses. An occasional Makah family still came to Ozette to camp and fish, but through most of the year the village stood abandoned. The roofs of houses were rotten with moss and caved in. Walls that once sheltered families lay broken and fallen in the grass. Obviously this had been a big village and an important one. There wasn't time to investigate carefully, but Daugherty made notes and took pictures, then hiked back through the wet forest to his car. The winter term was about to begin at the university. It was time to head back to the city.

Classes got under way, and over the next few years student life gradually changed into faculty life as work on a Ph.D. degree was completed. By 1950 September to June found Professor Daugherty teaching at Washington State University. Summers were spent excavating in the lava country of eastern Washington. Scraping the sunbaked earth of canyon bottoms and feeling dust stick to his sweaty skin, Daugherty often turned his thoughts to the cool coast of the Olympic Peninsula. However, dams under construction along the Columbia and Snake Rivers meant that hundreds of ancient Indian sites were sure to be lost, and lost soon. The salvage archaeology was urgent.

The year 1958 brought a brief return to the coast for investigations at Toleak. Then in 1961 came the chance to go to White Rock. Waves battering the beach there were washing out midden. Daugherty finished directing an archaeology field school and headed west with a crew. The traces of man's past were being lost to nature on the coast, as they were being lost to dams in the eastern part of the state.

There was only a month to dig before classes would begin again, but work went well. To judge by the great number of bones that lay in the deposits, hunters must have camped at White Rock year after year to go out after whales and seals. Daugherty couldn't yet be sure how long ago. Discoveries were very much like what the crew had found at Toleak, although that site seemed more recent. Additional sites would need to be studied before dates could be known and the full prehistory of the coast really understood. Maybe Ozette held the key. Daugherty decided to hike up and have another look. Fourteen years had passed since he had checked the remains of the old village there.

Morning dawned sunny and warm. Daugherty and two of his students shouldered packs and shovels and started up the beach. They passed petroglyphs of whales, pictures chipped into rock by Indians. Some were killer whales, easy to recognize by the high fins in their backs. Another seemed to be a gray whale, evidently a female because the Indian who pecked

the design into the rock had added a baby whale inside the abdomen.

Soon a high bank, green with ferns, came into sight, and Ozette lay just ahead. The three men walked thoughtfully along the beach and climbed over the logs tossed by high-tide waves. There was the broad, grassy terrace where the village had stood. Nettles brushed their trouser legs and stung their arms as they dug sample pits to test for remnants of human occupation. Midden seemed to be everywhere, and it was deep.

Ozette was the place to dig.

Left: Indians pecked petroglyphs into rocks
near Ozette. Nobody knows how old they are.

II
DIGGING
THE TRENCH

Four years passed, and research elsewhere kept Daugherty away from the Washington coast. He joined other archaeologists working in Egypt and Sudan to preserve evidence of man's past along the Nile River where the Aswan Dam was rising. Excavations in eastern Washington also continued, including discoveries in an isolated canyon where a site known as Marmes Rockshelter is located. Excavations there ultimately were to yield one of the longest sequences of man's occupation yet found in the western hemisphere—human bones 10,000 years old, dating from not long after the close of the last ice age. It was the summer of 1966 before work at Ozette could get under way.

The archaeology camp for the first season's
work lay just back from the beach.

The National Science Foundation had approved funds, and
a crew of twenty-five men and women studying archaeology
in colleges and universities across the United States and
Canada had come to learn field techniques and, in the process,
help unlock the story of Ozette's past. Camp was among the
trees and ferns just back from the beach where a splashing
creek furnished water for drinking and for icy showers. Meals
were eaten out on the beach, sitting on the drift logs or in a
big tent when the weather was bad. A Coast Guard helicopter
had airlifted equipment and supplies to get the project started.
There were shovels and surveyor's transits, groceries, a cook-
stove, tents, catalogs, and field-record books with the pages

The advance crew unloaded equipment from the helicopter.

still blank—everything needed for a hardworking crew of students and professors. Nearly four tons of material had come in at the outset, and now supplies had to be packed down the trail on the backs of students or flown in by light plane from the logging town of Forks, twenty-five miles distant. Often it was too foggy for the plane to land. For the same reason it wasn't always safe to travel down the rocky coast by boat to Lapush, the nearest village, eighteen miles away.

Daugherty had specific goals for the summer's work. Archaeology isn't just digging in the ground and finding things; that would result only in accumulating things, and the goal of prehistoric archaeology is to study relationships between things and the people who made them and used them. It is piecing together what man's life was like during the long years before there were written records.

First on the list of goals was to learn the physical size of the site and also how far back in time it reached. Makahs had kept on living at Ozette for nearly a century after white men began to settle on the Olympic Peninsula. Then a new government ruling required all Indian children to be in school, yet from Ozette the nearest one was fifteen miles up the beach in Neah Bay. Families began moving there, and by the 1930's Ozette stood empty. Daugherty knew the end of the story. He wanted to find the beginning. What was more, he needed to sample the evidence of the whole story and get a broad outline of what had happened at this one location through thousands of years. Later he could study individual chapters.

How to begin? An archaeological dig calls for an advance plan of action, and Daugherty had one. Human life at Ozette had not been an isolated phenomenon, and therefore more than man's story alone needed to be investigated. The Indians had lived in relation to the land and to the plants and animals. For this reason experts in geology and biology on the staff at the Washington State University Laboratory of Anthropology were to work right along with the students and

Geologist Fryxell discussed the excavation with Daugherty.

archaeologists. Carl Gustafson, a zoologist, had headed the advance crew that set up camp. Roald Fryxell, a geologist, would help Daugherty direct the dig and coordinate the work of specialists in fields outside archaeology.

Together the men picked the place to start excavating. It was a point of land that rose as a hillside above the beach—but not an ordinary hillside. A reef and islands not far offshore protect its slope from the full force of the ocean waves, and midden lies deep and undisturbed, not cut into by surf as it had been at White Rock. From the depth of the midden it was apparent that men had lived there for a long time, and the protection of the slope gave promise that the geologic record had been preserved along with man's record. Fryxell

Right, top: Ozette as seen from the air. *Bottom:* From the island, the village and its calm waters lie to the right, while the surf breaks on the unprotected beach at the left.

could trace a series of steplike terraces that somehow must relate to a changing level of the sea at this location. The uppermost stands about fifteen meters higher than the present beach. The oldest evidence of man probably would lie there, since the lower land would still have been underwater when man first came to Ozette.

The professors decided to start at today's beach and dig a trench up through the terraces. That would give them a

Daugherty discussed the progress of the excavations with Field School students.

sample of the full time range of the hillside. The work seemed slow at first. Nettles and salmonberry had to be whacked out of the way, and even after excavating began nobody could just dig. Every shovelful of midden had to be sorted through to see what it held. When something was found, its exact location and description had to be recorded. Even so, by the middle of July the trench ran forty-four meters up the slope.

Standing in the trench, Daugherty spoke to the students. "This kind of site is as difficult as any you'll ever dig," he told them. "You may feel you want to dig fast and find things, but that's not archaeology. This site is being destroyed as we work. We can never put it back together and come for a second look, so as we go along we need to record exactly what the deposits are like and what they contain."

Students worked as partners. One shoveled, carefully skimming the layers of the deposits. He or she tossed midden up onto a table, and there the second student checked through it with a hand trowel. When that was finished, a call of "Ready" would send up the next shovelful. Broken pieces of glass and dishes kept showing up in the surface layers. So did rusted nails, coins, part of an old-fashioned muzzle-loading rifle, and two beautiful doll heads made of china. These items belonged to the last years that Indians had lived at Ozette, and older layers within the earth proved similarly varied in content. There were fishhooks made from sharpened slivers of bone, attached to stones that acted as sinkers. There was a haircomb carved from bone and decorated with a man's face, and knife blades of shell and stone, together with whetstones used to shape and sharpen them. By the end of July more than two thousand items had been found, cleaned,

Following pages: Students carefully skimmed the deposits, tossing midden on tables to be sorted. Tags in the trench wall mark the exact levels at which artifacts were found.

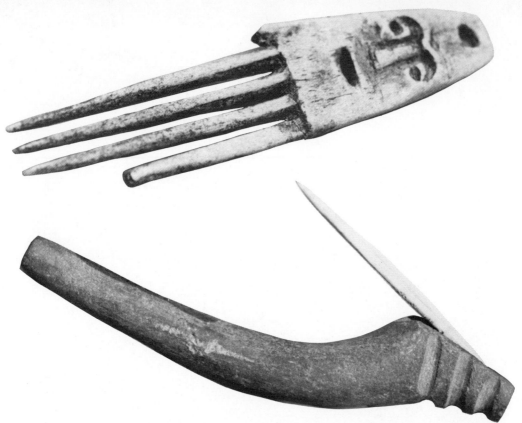

Top: Decorative comb made of bone. *Bottom:* Fishhook fashioned by lashing a bone point to a stone shank which also serves as sinker.

numbered, and described in the field catalog. A single day turned up seventy-two separate artifacts in the deposits as the trench lengthened and deepened still more. That particular day the crew found three bone points, a small chopper of slate, a stone knife of the kind used to cut bone, a whetstone, and a pile of sixteen points from fishhooks. Discoveries kept coming so fast that by afternoon students almost began to complain. "Another point," one teased her partner. "If you don't quit digging them up, we'll have so many notes to write that we'll never get to dinner."

Each artifact was washed and admired, and if it seemed unusual it was examined by Daugherty or the assistant archaeologist, Harvey Rice. Everything was saved, usual or unusual. "The field isn't the place to decide what's important and what isn't," Daugherty explained. "You do that later, after all the pieces are in and you can compare them and

Daugherty gently washed an artifact in the field lab.

think about them. Archaeology here calls for digging three months, then spending the rest of the year trying to understand what you've found."

No one type of training can give enough knowledge to understand a site fully, which is why the team of experts was working at Ozette. An archaeologist needs to know about plants, animals, geology, soils, fossils, and a dozen other sciences as well as to know about man. He needs to, but he can't. There isn't time enough in a single life to learn that much. Teamwork is the only answer, and Washington State University is unusual in having specialists in various sciences working and teaching together within the Department of Anthropology. Professors in other departments, of course, stood ready to help too. Many tests would be needed.

A part of understanding Ozette's past was to know what kinds of plants formerly grew there. This called for collecting samples of earth from the trench and from other parts of the site to be sorted through for grains of pollen. They would be studied under the microscope of a palynologist, a botanist who specializes in identifying pollen to determine past vegetation. Bits of wood might also serve as keys of this sort. They could be identified by characteristics of their cells.

With this sort of information Daugherty could answer questions, such as how long ago cedar trees had become available for canoes, and whether Indians in the past could have dried and stored the same kinds of fibers and berries as those used by Indians today. Knowing about the vegetation would even help to tell about the climate, since certain kinds of plants need particular temperatures and amounts of moisture in order to grow. If an archaeologist is going to understand peoples who lived by hunting and by gathering wild plants rather than by planting crops and raising animals, he particularly needs this sort of information. Farmers modify their surroundings, but hunters have to get along with whatever the land offers. At Ozette the evidence indicated that for thousands of years the climate had been about the way it is today, with the same kinds of plants and animals present.

Carl Gustafson could immediately identify many of the shells and bones coming from the trench. Clamshells and mussel shells were the most abundant, scattered everywhere in the trench except where so much time had passed that they had decayed. Most represented dinners from the distant past. Fish bones also lay scattered through the trench, from the surface to the deepest layers. Some were from kinds of fish that lived in the shallow water close to the village and would have been easy to catch. Others belonged to deepwater fish— and this meant that the Indians must have had boats and lines long enough to reach 100 to 150 feet below the surface.

Bird bones came from ducks, geese, gulls, shorebirds, and forest birds. A few fragments were charred and broken, which suggested that the birds sometimes were cooked and eaten. Eagle bones also were present, and Daugherty thought they probably were from birds hunted for their feathers.

Many layers of the excavation seemed practically paved with the bones of sea mammals. The huge whalebones got in the way. Ribs and jawbones often happened to be lying in such a way that they crossed the trench from one side to the other. They would be identified and photographed in place, then before digging could continue they had to be sawed in two and cleared away as if they were tree roots. Sometimes a whale vertebra was handy to sit on, and one shoulder blade stuck out of the excavation wall at just the right height to use as a table for writing up notes.

The farther the trench cut into the hill, the plainer it became that the people there had been well organized even in very early times. The bones alone proved this. They were as abundant in the old deposits as in recent ones, and since successful whale hunts demanded teamwork, the presence of the bones clearly showed a high level of organization among the ancient Ozettes.

"My dad used to pray and prepare himself for months ahead of whaling season," Daugherty was told by one of the Indian men he met while making his early studies along the coast. "He knew special songs to bring power, and he had magic amulets and charms that he kept in a secret place and wouldn't let the rest of us see. Sometimes he would swim out around the rocks beyond the surf, diving and spouting like a whale. He was pretending to be a whale to show that his heart was right. A man needed all the spirit power he could get when he led his crew on a hunt."

The whaler thrust his harpoon into a whale and prayed to the great animal's spirit, asking it to swim for the beach. "Our people will come to welcome you," he would say. "We will sing and dance and decorate your huge body with feathers." While the whalers were out, their wives and children in the village were helping too. They moved gently and talked softly as they went about the day because everyone knew that whales enjoyed coming to a quiet, orderly village.

Sometimes a harpooned whale headed for the open ocean

Right: The excavation cut up the hill, sampling the terraces and the centuries.

instead of toward the village beach. The men would know then that they had not prayed and prepared well enough, or that somebody in the village had neglected proper behavior. They knew too that they were in for an ordeal. They might have to follow the whale for more than a day. As preparation they carried water with them, inside bags of sealskin, and for food they took along dried fish and a little oil. A whale crew even carried fire. Glowing coals were put into matched clamshells, which were tied shut. A box with a layer of beach sand in the bottom and a few pieces of wood permitted them to build a fire right in the canoe.

As soon as the harpoon head sank into the whale's flesh, it locked there, mostly by turning sideways, or "toggling." It was not expected to kill prey so huge as a whale—or even a sea lion, seal, or sea otter. Its purpose was to restrain the animal. With toggling harpoons, the head is held onto the shaft by friction, and it comes off after being driven into the body. The shaft falls away, and a rope attached midway along the head causes the toggling.

In the case of a whale, men in the canoe did not hold onto the rope, for fear of being pulled overboard, but they had a system for gaining some control. As soon as they saw the harpoon head pierce the whale's side, they started throwing overboard a series of baskets that held coils of rope running from basket to basket. The coils paid out automatically, and the baskets could be picked up later. Six or eight floats made of sealskins and blown up like big balloons were tied to the rope. They made it hard for the whale to swim or to stay down when it dove. The wounded animal couldn't escape, and the pull of the floats was immensely tiring.

A second harpoon would follow the first, and soon more floats dragged in the water and pulled against the whale. Usually two or three canoeloads of men hunted together, and when those in one canoe sighted a whale they would raise a paddle into the air as a signal. They had the right to set the first harpoons, but after that, if they felt additional harpoons were needed, they called the other canoes to come alongside and help. Those men also thrust harpoons into the whale. Still more floats trailed from the additional ropes, and the drag increased.

Finally the animal would tire and lie exhausted on the surface, unable to dive anymore. A crewman in the first canoe would reach out with a razor-sharp lance of mussel shell and cut the tendons of the flukes. The whale no longer could swim, and it was safe to paddle close enough to drive in a killing lance behind the flipper. When it pierced the heart, the whale would roll, spout blood, and die.

A man from the first canoe then slipped overboard and swam to the mouth of the great beast. He cut slits in the lips and lashed the mouth shut. That kept it from gaping open and letting water fill the carcass, which would make it heavy or even sink it. The floats were brought up and tied on each side of the whale to help the body ride high and be easier to tow. A rope was attached to the jaw, and the proud paddle for home got under way. In high spirits the men sang special towing songs as they dipped their paddles into the water. The rhythm eased the work and shortened the miles.

Ozette was an ideal location for whale hunting. The shore is protected by the reef and offshore islands. Storms occasionally crash waves onto the beach, but for the most part the

The Ozettes cleared a dragway through the rocks
of the lower beach to facilitate landing their canoes.

ocean laps gently. Canoes could land in safety, and landing
is the most dangerous part of handling a small craft along the
coast. Going out through a surf rarely is too hard, but when
beaching, even moderate waves can cause swamping. Protected water is the greatest welcome a returning canoeist can
have.

Landing a whale required waiting for the incoming tide to
be full so that the carcass could be floated high onto the beach
and secured. When the tide went back out, there the whale
would be, convenient for cutting and dividing. A Makah
victory song brags, "The Makahs have no equal in numbers

Makahs stripped blubber from a whale on their beach
at Neah Bay. Photo taken in the early 1900's.

or strength. It is nothing for us to have forty whales on the
beach in a day. . . ."

This is an exaggeration. Two or three whales in a single
day would have been a remarkably successful hunt. But the
song shows how the people felt. Whaling meant far more to
Coast Indians than simply a supply of meat and blubber.
Much of the religious and social life of the village centered
around whaling. Prestige, wealth, and membership in certain
secret societies were involved.

Daugherty knew this from the early accounts he had read
and from talking with the Indian men. He felt that whale

hunting must reach far back into the misty and unknown past along the coast. There in the Ozette excavations was proof.

The Alaskan peoples that hunted whales did so in almost exactly the same ways as Indians along the Washington coast. Their boats were the same size (though the Alaskans used a framework covered with walrus hide instead of a dugout canoe). Whaling crews were made up of eight men in both places, the same sort of sealskin floats were used to tire the whale and weaken it. Harpoon heads followed different designs but functioned in the same way and were kept in the same sort of flat bags. Among both peoples, complex ceremonialism centered around both the equipment and the hunt. The similarities suggested that an understanding of prehistoric whaling might lead to understanding the culture of the northwest coast as a whole.

III
MORE PIECES
TO FIT TOGETHER

By mid-August the excavations stretched uphill for seventy meters and had cut through four meters of deposits. Each new layer within the earth represented a new page from the past.

An example of this came one day as Gustafson watched a student scrape with a trowel, carefully cleaning around a cluster of shells about the size and shape of golf balls cut in half. Whale barnacles! As tiny larvae they had attached themselves to the whale's skin and begun to build shells. From then on they traveled through the ocean wherever the whale swam, feeding—as the whale itself did—by filtering microorganisms out of the water. These particular barnacles were

51

Barnacles from the skins of whales
testify to the success of long-ago hunts.

a kind found on gray whales and humpbacks, which are
baleen whales with great curtains of fringed bone along their
lips, used like sieves to capture tiny creatures and plants from
the water.

Finding the barnacles, Gustafson knew that a piece of
whale skin once had lain on this exact spot. Probably a whale
had been floated onto the beach and butchered. Maybe this
was 300 years ago, or 500, or 5,000; nobody yet knew the
age of material in the trench. Indians would have gathered
around the sides of the whale and even up on top, cutting
with shell and bone knives. Somebody had sliced off a chunk
of blubber and carried it up into the village with the skin
still attached. Centuries later the barnacles were all that remained. Maybe the blubber was for an ordinary family dinner.
Maybe it had supplied oil for a party that included dancing
and singing and tales of the hunt.

Clusters of the barnacles showed up repeatedly as the digging went on. They were in all parts of the trench, especially the end near the beach.

Another story was becoming clear from the animal bones: people at Ozette hunted at sea much more than in the forest. Deer and elk are common on the Olympic Peninsula today, even right on the beach. Two deer visited the archaeology camp almost every evening, sometimes following students on their sunset strolls along the beach. Probably the animals were about as common in the past as now, and Ozette Indians could easily have used them as a main source of meat if they wished. Evidently they preferred not to. It was a rare day in the trench that anyone found a land-mammal bone. This did not prove the Ozettes never ate meat from deer or elk, for example, but it did seem to show that hunting land mammals had not been a major occupation.

Daugherty thought the Indians might have moved into the river valleys or mountains to hunt in the fall when elk gather in herds of 100 or more. If so, women would have stripped the flesh from the bones as the men brought in each day's hunt. Cut thin and dried, meat could be transported easily to the main village. Or Ozette Indians might have traded seal and whale oil to inland tribes for dried elk and deer meat.

Either way large numbers of bones from forest animals would not have found their way to Ozette and, therefore, couldn't be expected in the trench. A few may have been brought to the village to make into harpoon barbs and fishhooks, tool handles, and other implements. Land-mammal bone is heavy and dense and thus more suitable for tools than sea-mammal bone, which is light and porous.

One thing was sure. For every bone that came from a land animal there were dozens from ocean animals. This was true even without counting the whalebones, so big they had to be placed in a class by themselves. Clearly, the main hunting activity at Ozette had been for sea mammals. Combined with fishing, collecting shellfish, and gathering wild-plant foods, the ocean hunting had given the Ozettes a more guaranteed supply of food than farming tribes knew in other parts of the country. Not that hunting was easy even when it was for fur seals and sea lions, let alone for whales. Male seals weigh nearly 600 pounds; male sea lions up to two tons. Harpooning them demanded bravery and skill as well as strength, but the supply could be counted on. The Ozettes knew that fur seals and whales would come by the thousands each spring, that berries would ripen in summer, and that salmon would enter the river to spawn each fall. They didn't have to plant fields or tend crops or herd animals, yet their livelihood was as dependable as that of agricultural tribes. All they needed to do was harvest.

Indians alive today who still remember the old times say that the meat of fur seals is the most delicious of all, and sea-lion meat is the next best. This must be why Ozette was such a favorite location through the long centuries. No other point on the Washington coast reaches so far to the west, so close to the migration routes of fur seals. Gustafson asked men in the United States Fish and Wildlife Service to check back as far as their records went and let him know where fur seals had been seen along the coast. He put a pin on the map for each sighting and found that the route swung near to shore at Ozette. Along the rest of the Washington coast the seals stay ten to fifty miles offshore, a long way for hunters to paddle. But at Ozette a reef just three miles from the beach teems with fish that seals feed on. Hunters usually needed to go only that far. Each spring the herds passed the village on their way to the arctic waters off Alaska and Siberia, where the females would give birth to their pups and feed for the summer, building thick layers of fat. Then they would start south again toward their winter feeding grounds off the coast of Oregon and California. The spring migration was the most

Sea lions bask in the sunshine on a rocky islet a short distance offshore from Ozette.

concentrated. A hunting crew could hope to take as many as a dozen fur seals in a day anytime from March through May.

As work in the trench proceeded, each area to be excavated was marked off with white string into two-meter squares, and each square was numbered. When a bone or artifact was found it was put into a paper bag and labeled with the number of the square it came from and the depth within the deposits. Such exact documentation is vital. Otherwise an archaeologist won't have a complete record of the layers and cannot relate the position of one discovery to another.

To find the age of the different levels within the site, Daugherty and Fryxell planned to have charcoal from fire hearths tested for radiocarbon content. This is a special form of carbon produced as cosmic rays from outer space bombard the earth's atmosphere and change a tiny fraction of the nitrogen into radioactive carbon, also called carbon 14, or simply C^{14}. This carbon is unstable and begins to break down as soon as it is formed.

Plants pick up C^{14} from the air, and animals get it from the plants they eat as food. When an organism dies it stops taking in this carbon, but what already is in the tissues continues to decay and ultimately disappears. Working with special equipment, nuclear physicists can measure the amount that is left, and comparing this to the known rate of breakdown they can figure how many years have passed since the plant or animal died. Charcoal makes the best samples. It gives fairly accurate counts for ages from 300 to 35,000 or 40,000 years.

Dozens of samples would be needed from the trench. If results from testing them were consistent with each other, the layers within the deposits could be given ages in terms of years. If there just wasn't enough material to feel safe in using radiocarbon dating, relative dating would be used instead. For example, sometimes an archaeologist has no way to know exactly how old a particular layer is, but he does know that it is more recent than the one below. In this way, even without learning the actual age of any of the layers, he can figure out the order in which events occurred. This helps in understanding a site, and by comparing the layers of deposits and their artifacts in one site with those from other sites in the same region, something of the prehistory of the people can be told.

For recent deposits there is another way of figuring out dates. At Ozette the upper layers obviously belonged to the years after white men had arrived on the coast. Coins were present. They had to have been dropped later than the dates stamped on their faces, since obviously they couldn't have been lost before they were made. Furthermore, whatever lay beneath them must have been there longer than the coins were, and anything above must have accumulated after the money was dropped. In a similar way the manufacturing date of certain kinds of dishes and glass bottles can be traced. So can styles of buttons and buckles, types of rifles, and fittings from ships.

Cardboard trays filled with such items were stacked on the lab shelves along with trays that held prehistoric material—pieces of sharpened shell, beaver teeth made into a sort of dice, and bone that had been carved into fancy haircombs. When something broken was found, Daugherty or one of the students in the lab glued it together and set it in a tray filled

Each artifact was numbered and cataloged.

with sand to support it gently and evenly while the glue dried. By early August more than 4,000 artifacts had been cleaned and cataloged, and an extension to the lab sheltered the whale-bones and the bags of smaller bones.

By the summer's end, radiocarbon dates had not yet been run from the oldest parts of the site, but the tests that were complete indicated at least 2,000 years of human occupation. Furthermore, artifacts showed that during all those centuries

The trench had yielded artifacts ranging from tools 2,000 years old to modern cartridges, beads, and numerous other items.

hunting and fishing activity had changed very little. The trench had been a test excavation to give a sample of what the site held. "It's been a window to the deposits," Daugherty summed up the excavation. "Now we can know what level to investigate in order to learn about a particular period. We'll peel off layers from a broad area of midden and look for what's left of houses as well as for artifacts and debris that has been dumped. The trench has been a beginning."

IV
GEOLOGICAL
EVIDENCE

Part of Roald Fryxell's job was to study the relationship between the individual strata, or layers, of the excavation. He described his work as sitting and staring at the black mud walls of the trench until they began to make sense.

"It's like looking at people's faces in a crowd," he said. "They all look the same at first. Then you start noticing different characteristics, and after a while you recognize individuals. The layers of the midden are that way too. They look like nothing but mud with pieces of shell and bone at first. Then you find what to watch for, and individual stories begin to show up."

One of the problems Fryxell worked on was the matter of

relative dating. Layers in a midden seldom are distinct, and this gives archaeologists trouble in piecing together the sequence of what has happened. Daugherty and Fryxell felt this needn't be the case. Geologically, the layers had to be present since the deposit had built bit by bit through the years. The record must be there. The problem was to read it.

By watching each day as the trench deepened and lengthened, Fryxell knew the step-by-step opening of the earth from a geological standpoint. The cross section of the hillside was

Fryxell studied the layering of the midden deposits.

like a slice through time. Surface layers held the roots of today's plants, and mixed in with them were rusted nails and broken dishes. Depending on where you stood along the trench, the next layers might include twenty-five or thirty centimeters of broken clamshells and mussel shells from long-ago feasts, a whale rib, or fur-seal bones and fish vertebrae. There might be a band of snail shells, then a pocket of charcoal or red-brown sand and fire-cracked rock left from an ancient cooking fire. Tags marked levels where artifacts had been found. At the very bottom would be layers of silt and clay seemingly associated with ice-age glaciers before man's arrival.

In places it was possible to pick out where a house had stood. The thin layering of soil and sand and debris from the packed-earth floor still showed, and postholes were plain, filled in with sediments different from those of the surrounding deposit. Sometimes there were decayed bits of wood, evidently all that was left of the posts. In the very bottom of the trench the crew uncovered a hearth. Three meters of midden had built up on top of it, a steady accumulation that must have taken centuries. Nothing pointed to long periods without human occupation or indicated waves or rainstorms ever having washed away parts of the deposits. Logs or wooden planks may have been used at times to build seawalls that helped protect the village site, and at least once a breakwater of stone had been used. Part of the wall was exposed in the trench cross section.

This seawall together with features such as the hearths, postholes, and floors became pieces of the archaeological puzzle right along with the bones and artifacts and the thin,

The students took measurements and made
scale drawings of the excavation walls.

individual layers of midden. The purpose of the excavation
was to find as many such pieces as possible and fit them together. Careful records were kept so that the study could continue after the trench walls had slumped and grown over
with plants.

Each student wrote notes detailing what he found as the
scraping and digging went along, and he also made a scale
drawing of his particular section of the excavation wall. Layers as fine as two centimeters thick were included. So were

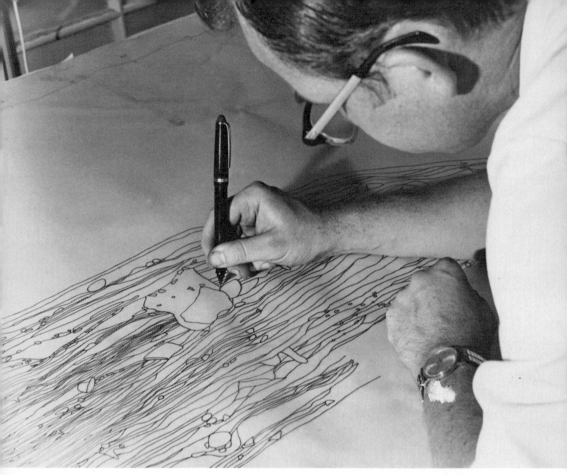

Combined into one, the drawings showed layering of the deposits, stones, and holes where the house posts had been.

stones and the deposits of sand and the whale bones, the post-holes and hearths. Seldom before had such a complete picture of midden been put together. When the separate drawings were combined, the sheets of paper stretched twenty feet for each wall of the trench.

In addition to the drawings, actual samples of the excavation wall were saved as a part of the record. The crew soaked a glue-like vinylite resin into vertical sections about twenty centimeters wide to make them hold together. When the resin dried, they set a board against the face of each section and carefully cut and tied the stabilized column onto it with strips of cloth. The technique had been developed by professors of soil science at Washington State University, and Fryxell had adapted it to archaeology as a way of providing permanent records of an excavation. The columns, or "monoliths," formed a sort of library that could be studied in detail at any time back in the Laboratory of Anthropology. Twenty such columns were taken from the trench walls.

An overall understanding of the coast's geology still had not become clear. If anything, it seemed to grow more complex as the summer went on. Yet deciphering the geology was the only way to know when the land had become available for man to liv on. During the maximum stage of the last ice age, about 14,000 years ago, a glacier nearly half a mile thick covered part of the Olympic Peninsula, and Ozette may well have been sheathed beneath ice that reached out into what now is the ocean. Along the beach, scratches in the bedrock record the paths of rocks that ground their way westward held at the bottom of the ice, and there also are blocks of granite and other stone that inched along with the glacier. They range up to the size of an automobile, brought to the coast, probably from Canada, as the ice advanced, then dropped when it melted. You find them now on the beach and in the forests and mountains of the Olympic Peninsula to about the 3,000-foot elevation. Gravel, clay, and silt also rode with the ice. Deposits of these sediments from three to seven meters thick cap the tops of several offshore islands.

Geologists agree on this basic part of the Olympic coast's past, but what happened after the ice melted is less easily understood. Some geologists have thought that as the enormous weight of the glacier was released, the land slowly rose from the ocean. Others suggest that melt from the ice must have flooded into the ocean and raised the water level. Still others point out that the Olympic Mountains may even now be wrenching upward from the earth's crust, lifting the Pacific edge of the Peninsula with them even though the eastern side quite clearly is dropping. A great plate of land might be tilting, causing one edge to rise while the other lowers. Fryxell checked the evidence.

What today is beach must have been underwater in the past. And what now are terraces back in the forest probably at one time were beaches where Indians could have landed their canoes. On the hillside at Ozette, Daugherty and Fryxell had counted four or five distinct terraces reaching as high as fifteen meters above the present beach. This was before they even began to excavate, and as Fryxell continued to look he found more. The men had hoped the terraces would prove to be a sequence that marked the coast's rise from the ocean. If so, the highest terrace would be the oldest. It would be the place to search for the earliest evidence of man.

Material in the trench seemed to bear this out. Shell and bone on the upper terrace were almost entirely rotted and gone, exactly as would be expected with the passage of a great length of time. A dark stain was about all that remained. Also, tools found there seemed cruder than those from the lower, possibly younger terraces—although Daugherty could not say so with confidence until the high terrace had been excavated more extensively, and this would be a slow job. Whatever knives or other tools of shell and bone the

Indians may have had were no longer present. They had rotted. So had all the wooden and fiber objects. Only stone was left. Certainly it represented just a fraction of the variety of tools the people actually had, and therefore it made a poor basis on which to judge their culture.

Fryxell could not say what the geology of the site had been either, until he had more time to investigate. He wanted to decode the order of geologic events, but as the weeks went by he realized the story was more complicated than he had expected. A steady rising of the land had not occurred, as most geologists had believed. Probably this has been the overall trend of geologic events along the coast since the close of the last ice age, but it has been a rise with many ups and downs. Through the long ages, the land and the ocean repeatedly have shifted in relation to each other.

One of the terraces that the trench cut through about two thirds of the way up the hillside held telltale evidence of age. Sand lay far below today's surface. Instead of being all fine grains, this sand had so much coarse material mixed in that it could not have been windblown. Fryxell collected samples and made tests by shaking the sand through a series of screens, each one finer than the mesh above it. Pebbles and shells caught in the first screen, gravel and broken shell in the next, and so on down to fine sand, which sifted through most of the series. Similar shaking and sifting was done with samples from today's beach and from the old beach buried beneath the midden. Then Fryxell compared results.

The percentages of coarse material in relation to fine sand and silt were about the same for all three. This was as expected. The terrace definitely must be an old beach from

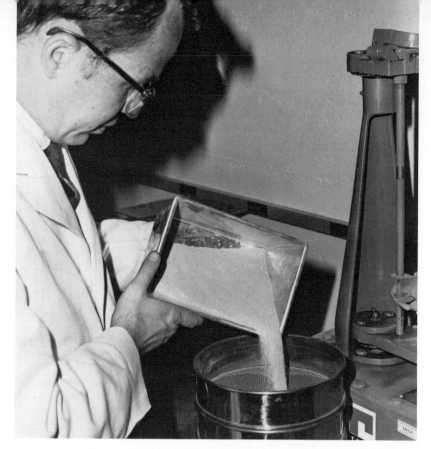

Fryxell analyzed sand from the terraces and the beach.

sometime in the geologic past. Knowing how old would make it possible to know more about when man might have built his houses at Ozette and towed ashore his whales. Charcoal from a terrace lower than this one had dated by radiocarbon as between 1,400 and 1,500 years old. Certainly the terrace with the old beach sand was older than that, but until much more material for radiocarbon dates was found, it would be impossible to say how much older. Quick, simple answers would be satisfying and helpful to work with, but real understanding seldom comes so easily. Apparently the project was going to take prolonged study. Only then could the history of

Daugherty and Rice used an auger to test for cultural deposits.

the earth be discussed in relation to man's arrival and early living situation.

Field school ended and a small crew stayed on, working in the area surrounding the trench. Daugherty and Rice made tests with an auger that could drill down into the earth and bring up samples of what lay hidden from sight. Did the midden continue far beneath the surface? What about hearths and other signs of houses? Throughout the day the whine of the auger powered by a chain-saw motor rose above the cry of the gulls and the lapping of the waves. The men were working in a tangle of sword fern and elderberry overtopped by alder trees. Each time the auger chewed a new hole one meter deep it gave them another look into the earth.

"Sand. We must have an old beach here," would be the comment one time. The next time, "We got water in this one."

"Rock. A layer of cobbles here."

"We're in a bone pile this time. Whalebones."

Sampling parts of the site beyond the slope with the trench was another of Daugherty's goals for the summer, and these first investigations seemed so promising that arrangements were made for the Air Force to fly in a core drill that could be used to bring up actual samples of deep deposits. This way the layering within the earth could be studied, and although the drill might cut into buried objects, the risk was worth taking. Information gained from the cores would guide future excavations and quite possibly prevent damage that might otherwise be done by working down blindly through the deposits.

Fryxell, Gustafson, and two or three students stayed on after Daugherty and the others had returned to Pullman. Each day they whacked brush out of the way and dragged the heavy rig along one of the terraces above the beach, collecting evidence. They took eleven cores. The drill cut through the roots of today's plants, through midden, and down to bedrock almost seven meters below the surface. The men could feel the drill hit the rock. It quit biting deeper, and when they brought up the core they found chips of rock.

Almost everywhere they were working beneath the water table. The first two cores contained midden that looked practically fresh, although it came from far below the surface.

In the trench, material from a similar depth had been mostly rotted. Here it was well preserved, and Fryxell noticed that mud, seemingly from a slide, lay on top of it. Farther down he found more mud and another layer of shell and bone fragments. A few shreds of wood were mixed in, which was even odder since plant fiber usually rots in a very few years.

Fryxell searched through the jungle of brush and mapped the evidence of all the mud slides he could trace on the present surface. He drove stakes into a few and recorded their exact position so that he could measure them again the next year

Fryxell checked the drill cores for color and texture.

and find out whether the slope was continuing to move. Then he and Gustafson and one last graduate student wrapped the core samples in plastic to send back to the Laboratory of Anthropology. The cores were wet and not held together with resin like the monoliths, yet they had to be kept in one piece or the record would be lost. It was like wrapping wet noodles four inches thick.

By early October the work was done. All the samples were ready, and the three men waited for the little plane that would fly them out along with the last of the equipment and discoveries. Cow parsnip plants beside the trench had grown nine feet tall and turned brown. Winter rains had begun, and overhead vees of geese were flying south. The season was over.

V
PHONE CALL
FROM THE MAKAHS

Back on the Washington State University campus classes began again, and the work of analyzing the materials and records from the field got under way. Daugherty worked on
plans for continuing the dig, including the problem of raising
funds. Harvey Rice and other graduate students sorted artifacts. Fryxell cleaned the monoliths and prepared them for
permanent storage.

Gustafson classified the animal bones from the trench—
80,000 of them, not including the whalebones. Even with the
help of an assistant, it took six months just to get them sorted
by type. After that, Gustafson traveled to Washington, D.C.,
and spent weeks taking measurements from bones in the col-

Students labeled artifacts *(above)*, Fryxell worked
with the monoliths *(right, top)*, and zoologist Gustafson
identified the animal bones *(right, bottom)*.

lections of the Smithsonian Institution. These would help
with identification of the Ozette collection. Often he could
tell what kind of animal a bone came from simply by looking.
Its overall size and shape were enough. Others Gustafson
recognized by how muscles or tendons had been attached, or
by measurements of how joints had fit together.

More than 90 percent of the bones from the trench proved
to be sea mammal, even without counting the whalebones.
Eighty percent were fur seal, and since these bones came as

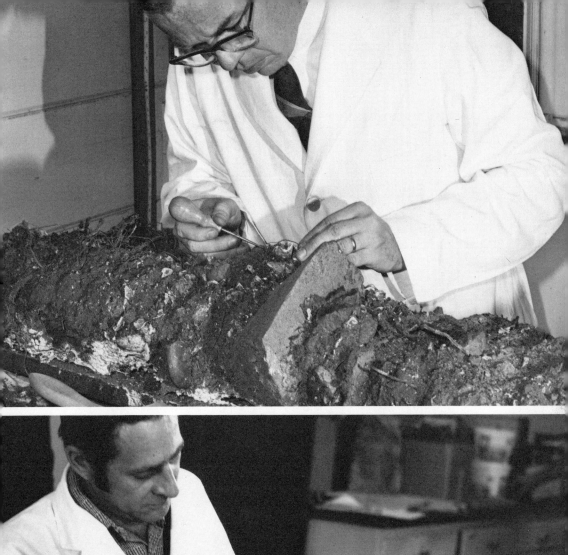

abundantly from the older parts of the site as from the recent levels, it was plain that Ozette Indians must have been canoe Indians from the earliest times. Fur seals don't come ashore except on their breeding grounds. The only way to hunt them is from a canoe.

When summer came Daugherty and Fryxell again held field school at Ozette, this time excavating a slope not far from the trench. Photographs of Ozette taken in the 1890's showed a dozen houses lined up just back of the beach, and the goal for the summer was to study this evidence of the recent village. Students also would check the top of the Cannonball Island, so close offshore that it is joined to the beach by a sandspit at low tide.

Surprisingly, midden on top of the little island proved nearly three meters deep. Through the centuries Indians had climbed the steep trail carrying up baskets of clams from the beach, fish brought in by canoe, and meat from fur seals. Daugherty thought perhaps they retreated to the island when warriors from other villages threatened raids, or maybe they used its height as a lookout post to watch for whales.

Work went smoothly and routinely in the excavation of the historic houses, with an abundance of items such as broken dishes and glass bottles being found along with stone and bone tools, bits of clamshell and mussel shell, and huge whalebones. There were also parts of rusted rifles and miscellaneous iron fittings from a ship, probably the barque *Austria,* which was wrecked on the reef fronting the Ozette village in 1887 during a winter storm. Its anchor still lies among the rocks exposed at each ebb tide, and part of the hull rests half buried in the sand of the upper beach. The

Left: Great quantities of whalebone in the midden gave evidence of the importance of whale hunting to the Ozettes.

Ozettes had adapted some of the iron from the ship to their own needs. Students also found iron axe heads used as wedges, in place of the old-style wedges of elk antler or hardwood, a knife blade hammered out of a leaf from an automobile spring, and an awl, or punch, fashioned from a nail.

A wet area at the edge of the beach yielded surprising treasure—rope twisted from cedar or spruce twigs, torn mats of cedar bark, and several baskets. All were well preserved, and this was astonishing considering how quickly plant fiber tends to rot. Evidently the material had lain constantly in the wet clay, and this had sealed off air and given protection against attack by bacteria and fungi.

In a muddy area up the hill an even more exciting discovery was under way. Daugherty wanted to sample how far back from the beach the cultural deposits extended, and so a crew had dug test pits away from the main excavation. One had gone nearly three meters deep and showed signs of becoming dangerous. Water seeped into it from upslope and softened the sides, threatening to collapse them. But just as Daugherty was about to call a stop, one of the students felt his shovel hit something solid. He probed by hand and found wood—a plank covered with a cedar-bark mat. Underneath it lay pieces of baskets and more planks, one of them ten centimeters thick and seventy-five wide. It had been split and finished by hand, but its edges were as beautifully squared as if cut with a power saw. Apparently a house had stood on this spot long ago, when what now was the bottom of the pit had been the surface of the hillside.

The wood was perfectly preserved. This fact, together with the sand and clay that lay on top of it, made Daugherty and

Fryxell think that a slide must have smashed into the house
and buried it, locking it immediately within the earth and
preventing decay. A number of such slides had occurred along
this slope, and as Fryxell checked the survey stakes he had
placed ten months before, he found that they were tilted.
There could be no doubt that the slope was still an active one,
with layers of wet mud oozing slowly and at times gathering
enough pressure to slide catastrophically. Makah families
have legends of mud sweeping into the village at Ozette,
knocking down houses and burying them so deeply that people
and possessions were lost forever.

Everything would still be in such houses. It would be like
a sudden stopping of time. One moment life had been going
on at its normal pace; the next instant it was sealed within
the earth. Think what could be learned by excavating such a
house! Daugherty yearned to check the pit further, but a
proper job would take months and time again was running
out. Such a house would be too valuable to work with on
anything less than a full-scale basis. Sadly, Daugherty ordered
the pit filled in. Summer was ending. Classes soon would
start back on the university campus. Funds were nearly gone.
Furthermore, urgent salvage archaeology in eastern Washington again demanded full attention.

Three years passed, and the calendar showed February,
1970, when Daugherty received a phone call urging him back
to Ozette. It came from Ed Claplanhoo, chairman of the
Makah Tribal Council at the time and formerly a student at
Washington State University. Storm waves driven high onto
the beach had undercut the bank at Ozette, Claplanhoo re-

Ed Claplanhoo, Makah tribal chairman when the buried
house was discovered, examined a killing lance for whales.

ported, and wet midden had slumped. Deep layers within the
bank now were exposed, and old-style fishhooks of wood and
bone, parts of inlaid boxes, and a canoe paddle had washed
out from where they had lain buried for centuries. Hikers
had found the artifacts. They were even carrying them away
—and once such items are gathered up and taken off by col-
lectors, they no longer reveal the life of the people who made
them and used them. They become mere things.

Daugherty listened to the Tribal Chairman's full account;
then he headed almost straight from the phone to his car. He
had to get to the coast and see for himself. If the discoveries
were as important as they sounded, he would need to raise

finances, hire a crew, round up the necessary field equipment, and begin excavating as soon as possible.

The drive took ten hours. Daugherty slept what was left of the night at the head of the trail and at dawn hiked the familiar three miles through the forest to the beach. Ed Claplanhoo and a delegation of Makahs met him. Together the men examined the slump—not a large one and completely without drama for most eyes. Banks along beaches the world over give way as a normal part of erosion. But Daugherty and the Makahs knew the special nature of this bank, and Daugherty even more than the others knew how much evidence of the coastal prehistory already had been lost. Sites mentioned in a 1917 report covering the Washington coast were nowhere to be found when he made his 1947 site survey as a graduate student. They had been swept into the ocean. Daugherty couldn't let this happen at Ozette. Not just as the preliminary work of 1966 and 1967 had given the keys needed to unlock the full archaeological story. The beginning of man's story at Ozette reached thousands of years into the past, and the site was extraordinary in also belonging to the modern day. Photographs show the last days of life in the village, and here on the beach with Daugherty were Indians whose families had lived at Ozette. People in Neah Bay could help the archaeologists understand the tools and household items certain to be found.

The slumped bank was about five meters high. Wild crabapple trees, elderberry, and sword ferns had slid with the mud and now formed a junglelike tangle. Daugherty climbed in among the roots and limbs, sinking over his boot tops in the ooze. His eye lit on planks that were sticking out end on, and a basketry rain hat of the kind women twined from spruce roots in the old days. There were also bone points used for shooting birds, halibut hooks, a harpoon shaft, and part of a carved wooden box.

Daugherty felt a familiar excitement. If this much had been brought to the surface, what must still lie hidden? Obviously these were the remains of a house. Not the one he had located in 1967. Another. How many more might lie buried with their contents preserved by the wet mud of the ages? How many of the missing pieces needed to understand the whale-hunting Indians of the Northwest lay beneath his feet? It was

Planks exposed by the slumping of the bank indicated the presence of a buried house.

as if the house had been delivered specially for study. A major expedition was needed, and right away.

Daugherty could not move to the coast immediately. Duties as chairman of the Department of Anthropology at Washington State University were too pressing. However, he recruited Gerald Grosso as operations manager to begin setting up camp. Grosso had worked along with the Ozette team from the first, helping in the 1966 trench and again the 1967 excavation. He knew archaeology, and he knew how to build cabins, plan a water system, and arrange for food and supplies four miles beyond the nearest road.

The next problem was money. The National Science Foundation had granted funds for the earlier work, but arranging financing through any foundation is a lengthy procedure. A research proposal must be submitted, evaluated by a panel of experts, and approved. There wasn't time enough for a formal application now. Waves were continuing to batter the beach, and too much material would be lost.

Claplanhoo called a meeting of the Tribal Council. Here was a chance for the Makahs to learn more about their own past, to see the kinds of things their parents and grandparents had told them about. Actual records of the tribe reached back only to the 1880's; and at that, they were a white-man's version of what Indian life had been like. Of course, tribal elders still told what they knew of hunting trips and houses and canoes, of legends and ceremonies. Dances and songs belonged to present-day Makah life, and families knew which spirits had given power to their ancestors. Indian names that had been in a family for generations were presented to Neah Bay young people on ceremonial occasions. Women still

Cedar bark for baskets and ceremonial
regalia is stripped from the trees.

talked husbands and sons into the heavy work of peeling
cedar bark from the trees so that they could weave baskets,
and each August the Makahs played host to nearby tribes
from western Washington and British Columbia, who came
for canoe racing, feasting, and dancing.

Right, top: Canoes used for racing are still hollowed
in the old way from cedar logs. *Bottom:* Boy wearing
cedar-bark headdress leads a dance on Makah Day.

Makah woman prepares salmon using split cedar
stakes similar to ones found in the buried house.

The tribe was proud of its heritage—so proud that this
chance to learn more excited them at least as much as it did
the archaeologists. The Council joined Daugherty in appeal-
ing directly to their senator, Henry M. Jackson. Through his
efforts $70,000 from the Bureau of Indian Affairs was trans-

ferred to the National Park Service and made available to carry the Ozette project through the summer.

At the site new excavation techniques were called for. Machines could not be used. The old house and its contents were too delicate. Not even hand shovels were possible. A metal edge would cut through a buried basket before even the most careful excavator could know it was there. Water seemed to be the answer. Pumped up from the ocean and blasted out through fire hoses, it would wash away the heavy mud on top of the house. Then the spray of garden hoses could be used when the crew reached the house and its artifacts. The method has decided advantages when working in saturated deposits. With a trowel, mud tends to ball up, and this may cause an archaeologist to scrape aside and lose small artifacts such as wooden arrow points, fishhooks, or shell beads. Working gently with water allows him to expose objects without disturbing them, and also the artifacts show up well because the mud has been washed off them.

Archaeologists in Washington had applied the technique to salvaging materials from a bog that a road was being built across, and Daugherty and Rice had used it at a river several miles from Ozette where baskets were showing up in the bank. The principle of excavating with water was sure, although putting it into practice was filled with headaches.

Tons of equipment were needed, and again the Coast Guard made airlifts. Later the Marine Air Reserve took over. The flights gave practice in loading and unloading all manner of materials—hoses, pumps, barrels of gasoline, lumber, roofing paper, stoves, propane tanks. Reservists could learn the

techniques of suspending heavy cargo under the belly of a helicopter and gain experience in the logistics problems of remote areas.

Even with materials in hand at Ozette, getting them into operation challenged ingenuity and patience. Time and again waves rolling in over the reef tore out the hoses that served the pumps, and a crewman would have to put on a wet suit and struggle out through the surging water to salvage what he could, then reset it all when calm had been restored. Sometimes seaweed clogged the pumps. Once stinging jellyfish spattered out of the hoses, burning and scarring Grosso's arms as he washed the mud from above the buried house.

By summer most of the problems were in hand. Hoses could deliver 250 pounds of pressure, and hydraulic excavation was begun on a scale never before attempted by archaeologists. Daugherty's strategy called for cutting through the upper layers as quickly as possible. It was tempting to check them in detail, but the 1967 excavation had sampled material that belonged to the years after white men appeared along the Ozette coast, and lots more from this period lay undisturbed on the terraces, available for later study. Getting down to the house was urgent, since waves already were washing into it.

Field school found archaeology students from across the United States converging on Ozette. They worked rain or shine, and really it made little difference what weather a day brought because the hoses splashed so much that everybody had to wear waterproof clothing anyway. Even school groups and families who had read of the dig and hiked out to see for themselves got spattered.

Left: Hoses were used to wash away
the deep mud covering the old house.

Students again worked as partners. One handled the hose; the other watched for anything that might wash out of the bank. The top meter or two of the deposits contained two thin layers with scattered bits of metal and crockery and also whale, seal, and fish bones. This was similar to what had been recovered during the 1967 dig, but beneath these midden deposits lay the heavy muck of the slide. It was a thick one. In places the streams of water from the hoses cut for nearly two meters through the mud.

Nobody could say what had caused the slide, although Fryxell's work made it plain that repeated slides were the rule at Ozette, and the Makahs' traditional tales of damage and tragedy bore this out. Daugherty thought this particular slide must have happened about 500 years ago. Nothing from the time of white men showed up as students searched the wreckage of the house, not even glass beads, which the earliest explorers and traders brought to the Northwest Coast beginning in the late 1700's. This meant the slide had struck before the time of contact with whites. Probably it was well before, because Indians traded items of white manufacture from tribe to tribe across vast distances long before they actually met the European newcomers face to face.

Evidently the slope had given away suddenly. Maybe it was at night when people were sleeping, for a few skeletons lay within the tangle of the house planks and furnishings. Perhaps there had been an instant of warning and other people had escaped. When human bones were found they were carefully gathered and taken to Neah Bay. The concern of archaeology is not with death, but with how people lived while their hearts beat and their minds and hands were busy. In time the Makahs would rebury the dead from the house, perhaps on the little hill behind the abandoned village, forever looking out on the rolling of the waves and the spouting of the whales.

Back in February, when Ed Claplanhoo first called Daugherty to come and look at the material washing out of the bank, the best guess was that excavating would take until September. Now September had come, and it was plain that the dig would go on. An archaeologist from the Smithsonian visited the site and told newspapermen he considered it "the most significant and unique find in Northwest Coast archaeology, truly a national treasure." A Canadian archaeologist from the National Museum of Man spoke of Ozette as "the most important archaeological site on the coast."

Daugherty joked that students could find so much in a single morning that they had to spend the next three days writing up discoveries and making scale drawings. These discoveries included a spruce-twig rope with a knot still tied in it, a club beautifully carved from whalebone, fancy wooden and bone combs for decorating hairdos, spindles for twisting fiber into cords, fishhooks, harpoons, paddles, boxes, all the wares needed for life on the coast five centuries ago were there in the house, and the work of uncovering them had barely begun.

The call from the Makah Tribal Council had initiated a project that clearly would take years to complete.

VI
THE OLD HOUSE

By December the winter rains already had been around long enough that the crew thought the whole world must be gray and wet. "Wind and rainstorm hit about 9 P.M. with gusts estimated at 50 knots," reads the informal daily logbook kept at the Ozette camp. "Windows rattled and buildings shook."

"Cool (33 degrees). About an inch of snow on the ground and the beach."

"Cool, hail, high winds. Snow flurries."

"We tried to hose the snow off the excavation so we could work. Results look like disaster at the sherbet factory."

Conditions were not comfortable, but excitement held. The project was like opening a time capsule. Here was an

Right: Careful excavation uncovered the walls, sleeping benches, and planks of the old house, scattered by the force of the slide.

Indian home from the time before Columbus set sail for America. Everything was present—sleeping benches, cooking hearths, storage boxes, harpoons, bows and arrows, baskets, mats, tool kits. All the household possessions of a family of whale hunters—and all of it tossed into a muddy jumble. The crew's job was to untangle the mess and discover its meaning. Find the roof planks and distinguish them from the wall planks. Hose away more of the mud slide and locate the north end of the house (so far work had been only in the south end). Keep notes and make drawings and photographs. Preserve each piece as it was lifted from the mud—the splintered boards the house was built of, the wooden bowls that once held seal oil and whale oil, the mussel-shell lance blades, the elk-antler wedges—everything.

This kind of a chance was practically unknown. Usually archaeologists must piece together the past from scattered indications such as weapons that got lost or were left behind as hunters shifted camp, or from household goods that had been abandoned when circumstances demanded moving on, or from refuse. Usually stone and bone is all that remains, as had been true in the trench at Ozette. There may be pottery too if the people belonged to a tribe that made pots, although Northwest Coast tribes used boxes made of wood instead of pots. One of their main cooking methods was by dropping fire-heated stones into boxes filled with water.

The house still held its original wooden and fiber materials, complete to wooden needles and pieces of string. There were even alder-tree leaves still green when first uncovered, although with exposure to the air they turned brown within seconds. Probably the house had been lived in for several generations,

Left, top: A notched roof support rests on the floor of the house where it fell when the slide hit. *Bottom:* Makah members of the crew look with pride at the careful adzing of the roof planks.

perhaps for a century or more. Parts of the wall showed damage from termites or carpenter ants, and the crew found several places where repairs had been made. A whalebone had been jammed in among the planks to close a break in the wall, and in another place part of a canoe paddle had been added as support. There was also a wide board that must originally have been intended as a roof board but was used in the wall. Parallel grooves ran the length of its surface, and these were how Daugherty recognized it as belonging originally to a roof. The purpose of the grooves was to direct rain runoff.

Sleeping benches were located next to the walls of the house. This one, being measured by Grosso, was nearly a meter wide.

The lower wall planks of the house's southwest
corner still stood, held in place by broken-off posts.

Some planks measured nearly a meter wide and were five
or six centimeters thick. Splitting them from cedar logs was
slow and hard, so householders naturally salvaged them whenever possible. An example of this was found in the house.
One of the largest planks was badly cracked but had been
repaired. Holes were drilled along each side of the crack, and
a cord was laced through them.

A crew of only four or five worked with Grosso. Daugherty

came out as often as work at the university permitted, and he planned to take leave as soon as possible and move from Pullman to Ozette. Money problems necessitated the small crew. Funds again had run out. The university supplied equipment and groceries, but the workers were without salary for the time being. School groups that came to see how field archaeology is done sometimes took up a collection to help with the financial crisis, and a state art society sent a donation. The dig was a chance to find wooden carvings from the Northwest older than those in any museum, since the house dated from long before white men had come to the coast exploring and collecting. Nobody interested in art could let such a chance to see the past slip away for lack of dollars.

Other donors came to the rescue too. Some gave their time by cooking or typing up reports so that the archaeologists could devote full energy to the excavation. The Makah Tribe sent groceries and arranged for high-school students to take time out from class and help at Ozette a few weeks at a stretch. Two gifts of $5,000 each came from wealthy businessmen in the state. The Marine Reserves continued helicopter service, and Congresswoman Julia Butler Hansen worked diligently to arrange proper funding through the National Park Service so that the research could go forward. Finally the message came that she had succeeded. Word was relayed by radio through the Coast Guard lightship beyond the reef, and the entry in the Ozette log for January 24, 1971, read, "Real celebration in camp tonight."

Discoveries came one on another. Some items were small and could easily have been missed or gone unrecognized except for the expert care being taken. There were finger-sized pieces of whittled wood that had been used as plugs in seal-skin floats. Several bone barbs from harpoons lay close by and with them were spirals of cherry bark, which had been wrapped around ropes made of sinew and fastened to the harpoon heads. The ropes had decayed and were gone, but the bindings remained. There was also a piece of bone roughed out and begun as a comb but never finished—the sort of find that archaeologists treasure because it gives both the article itself and a look at how it was made.

"Continued excavation in the house," reads the log. "Found several flattened wooden boxes in Square 70, Unit VI, one

Items as varied as the plug from a sealskin float *(left)* and an unfinished bone comb *(right)* were uncovered.

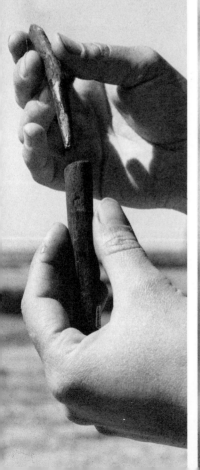

Inside a broken box a small plaid
blanket lay with a cedar-bark pouch.

with remains of what seems to be a blanket, white with blue-
black plaid design."

Something appeared to be folded inside, but Daugherty
gave orders against opening it, much as everybody wondered
what the contents would be. The blanket was so fragile that
the mud couldn't even be thoroughly cleaned off it, although
what inspection was possible seemed to show that it was made
of cattail fluff or the fuzzy seeds of fireweed. Perhaps dog
wool or mountain-goat wool had once been spun in with the
plant fluff, but it was gone now.

The crew wrapped the blanket in plastic to keep it moist,
then put it into a backpack. Three students headed down the
beach to the trail and began the long trip to the Laboratory
of Anthropology in Pullman. There they would see if X rays
would reveal the mysterious contents. If not, they would treat
the blanket with a mold preventative and put it into a freezer
for safekeeping. Seeing what lay inside was tempting, but not

worthwhile if unfolding the blanket would destroy it. The wrapping was unique; the contents might not be. No other plaid pattern was known along the Northwest Coast from such an early time. Daugherty wanted to save it even though it probably meant never knowing about the contents.

Tests seemed to bear out that fear. The X rays showed nothing. "It's like having a Christmas present you can't open," Daugherty said with a sigh.

On another day, not long after the blanket had been discovered, the entry in the log read, "Found a piece of carved wood set with teeth. Appears to be part of a feast bowl. Box removed from under it, also a canoe paddle."

Four days later the carving had been worked free and the log recorded, "Big wooden object assembled and photographed. It's not a bowl, but a carving in the shape of a whale's fin. Size, about eighty centimeters wide and eighty high with Thunderbird and other designs set in teeth and painted red and black."

The teeth were sea otter—700 of them. Most were molars, although there also were canines set in along the edge to give a jagged, saw-blade effect. A ceremony of some sort must have been associated with such an elaborate piece, but nobody could say what the rituals were or what importance the decorated fin held for the man who owned it. Written records make no mention of such an item, and none of the Makahs could remember their elders speaking of similar carvings. The only available clue came from an historical source. An etching made by the official artist for Captain James Cook's voyage of discovery in the late 1700's shows a carved fin in an Indian house on Vancouver Island, north of Ozette.

A whale fin carved of cedar was inlaid with more than
700 sea otter teeth. Those at the base were set in the design
of a mythical bird carrying a whale in its talons.

Baskets by the dozen were found in the old house. They
included storage baskets for dried fish and meat, burden baskets, clam baskets, and even hats woven like baskets. There
were also large, flat checker-weave baskets with harpoons in
them, and small woven pouches still holding bone points for

fishhooks and a whetstone to sharpen them on. Of special interest was a large carrying basket filled with rolls of bark that seemingly had been freshly stripped from a cedar tree, raw material for baskets or mats that never got made. The slide came before the bark had even been dried and put away properly. These are chores that Makah basket makers today take care of right away when they bring bark in from the forest, and probably the same was true in the past. If so, the slide must have come in May or early June, the only time for harvesting cedar bark because that is when sap rises and the bark peels easily from trees.

One basket seemed to be a kit. Somebody had finished work

Dale Croes, a graduate student studying the baskets, mats, and cordage of the site, cleaned a basket newly lifted from the mud.

one night and set it down; then centuries later Daugherty's and Grosso's hands were the next to touch it. Carefully the two men washed away the mud that had sealed the basket for so long. They lifted it from the jumble of house planks where it lay, and using the gentlest possible spray Daugherty began to free the contents. First to come out was a wooden whorl from a spindle, next two combs, one of them oddly fashioned with a double set of teeth. Awls were scattered through the basket, and there was a bundle of bird bones together with a whetstone, probably material intended for making more awls. Other items included stone blades, a lump of red pigment, and other clumps of indistinguishable fiber

The contents of a basket were gingerly
washed free and lifted out to be preserved.

Among the items in the basket was a double-ended comb artistically carved with a bear design.

perhaps intended for spinning into thread. Apparently this was a weaver's kit.

Operations were comfortably established by now in spite of occasional reminders of Ozette's wilderness location. A bear waking up hungry from hibernation broke into the cabins one night, and mountain-lion tracks printed the sandspit at Cannonball Island. The Marines continued to make flights except when storm or fog forestalled them, and food was also packed down the trail. The beach itself provided part of the crew's needs. Clams were dug at low tide, crabs were trapped on the reef, and strange goggle-eyed bottom fish were taken with hook and line.

Firewood for combating the damp cold of the winter came from the drift logs jackstrawed by surf on the upper beach—and cutting and hauling it to camp deepened the archaeologists' awareness of what life there was like for the Indians. Even with a power saw, garnering fuel took time and hard work. Daugherty began to think that the superabundance of logs brought to the beach by currents might be why certain

The archaeology camp, located beside the excavations,
had grown into a cluster of cabins built by the crew
from drift lumber, plywood, and hand-split shakes.

locations had been favored as camping places by early-day
Indians. Probably this was true at White Rock, the whalers'
campsite south of Ozette that he had investigated in 1961.
Also the position of the White Rock beach in relation to the
sun would have warmed it on winter mornings and lessened
the need for firewood.

The amount of work involved in getting fuel perhaps helped
to explain something else. Early photographs of Ozette showed
that the forest had been cut on Cannonball Island and also

Driftwood lining the beaches served as a source of fuel
and building materials for the ancient people of Ozette,
as for the archaeology crew who now live there.

behind the village. This clearing must have increased the in-
stability of the hill, and it probably contributed to the causes
of the mud slide.

By spring visitors occasionally numbered more than 100 in
a day. School classes from throughout Washington hiked out
to see the buried house. Indian people came from Neah Bay
and from as far away as the Yakima Reservation in eastern
Washington and various villages in British Columbia. A
physicist and his wife from Switzerland read about the Ozette

discovery in the newspaper there and came to the dig. Archaeologists from several universities and agencies walked the trail to watch the progress. By the summer of 1971, when excavation of the house had been under way just over a year and Daugherty had moved to the site to stay, some 20,000 people had slogged through the mud of the forest and dodged the lap of the waves on the beach to reach the site.

What a person saw depended on the stage of the excavation

Lying in the house wreckage was a carved plank
that must have been a decorative wall panel.

at the time, also on the individual. Crew members conducted tours and explained the archaeology. A display of artifacts gave a chance to look at what was found. Even so, standing on the bank and looking down into the house wreckage, the eyes at first seemed to take in little but blue-gray mud, hoses, and broken boards. But often there was more. For example, one of the planks was carved with a pair of wolves, or some other doglike animal, and a pair of birds with feather tufts

Wolves, or dogs, chased mythical birds across the panel.

on their heads. Perhaps the birds were a different sort of Thunderbird than is known from museum collections, or maybe they were a version of Owl, which has feather "horns" in some species. The plank lay now facing the sky and the spraying hoses of the archaeologists, but once it must have been a decorative wall screen.

If you watched where a student was hosing, you might see a fringed cedar-bark skirt washing free from the mud or

A whalebone with a blank for a club removed, a roughed-out club, and one that is finished show tools in all stages of manufacture.

One of the bowls for oil was carved in the form
of a man, finely detailed even to braided hair.

simple flat sticks used as tongs to lift hot stones from fire to
cooking box. A length of whalebone only partly shaped into
a club might be the beginning of a club similar to the beautifully carved and finished one found weeks earlier. A wooden
bowl could turn out to be delicately carved when it was
cleaned in the field lab. One such bowl still had red paint
faintly showing within, and another was shaped in the form
of a man. Two bowls actually still smelled of seal oil.

Stakes driven into the earthen floor had been the supports
for the wide sleeping platforms that ran around the wall of
the entire house. One set of them was angled and broken,
showing the direction the mud slide had come from and its
sudden, catastrophic force. In a back corner, near these stakes
and near where the wall screen had been, there was a wooden
box nearly the size of an apple box. It lay barely visible amidst
a jumble of wallboards, and broken against its corner were
two arrows. They seemed to have been snapped by the rush
of the slide. When the box finally was worked free and
opened, it was found to contain materials for making fish-

Paul Gleeson, project assistant director, pointed to bench
supports bent over by the force and weight of the mud slide.

hooks. There were bits of bone, a whetstone, fine cord wound
around sticks, and also finished hooks.

Detailed notes and drawings were kept as the work pro-
gressed. Always the backbone of an archaeological dig, in
some ways they had an added importance at Ozette. Discoveries there came in unusually rich array, and, with the
excavations stretching over a period of years, the makeup of
the crew shifted from time to time. Only careful records could
give a full sense of continuity. So many artifacts and parts
of the house itself were being recovered that by fall Daugherty

Madge Gleeson made a scale drawing
of the broken remains of the south wall.

shifted Grosso to increasingly full-time preservation work,
and Paul Gleeson, one of the graduate students, joined in
helping direct excavations, preparatory to heading the field
crew at the site when Daugherty's leave from the Washington
State University campus would be over and he would have
to return to Pullman. Gleeson had worked at Ozette in 1966
as the trench was dug and had worked with Daugherty in
eastern Washington. Now he was back earning his Ph.D. degree.

By the time field school began in the summer of 1972, the

size of the house was known at last. As the planks and household wares were found their position was documented and
they were put into preservation tanks as soon as possible. The
whole process of discovery and preservation was so pains-
taking that removal of the mud overlying the house went
slowly. The south wall had been washed free first, but it took
two years to work methodically toward the opposite end of

Structural remains of the house were placed in preservation
tanks when they were removed from the excavation.

the house and locate the north wall. When completely uncovered, the house measured an astonishing twenty-one meters
long and fourteen meters wide. This is larger than average
suburban houses today. Probably from twenty to forty people
had lived in it, all of them related but with individual family
units centering their living around separate cooking hearths
and sleeping platforms. The pattern was something like a

As each artifact and piece of the house was
lifted out, its exact position was recorded.

Each item was carefully cleaned before it was placed in preservative.

family apartment house with hanging mats and low walls as partial partitions.

June brought the most concentrated finds yet. They came from the northeast corner of the house, the opposite end from where the screen carved with the pairs of unidentified birds and canines had been found. The first hint was lengths of wood split off the edge of a plank. As students in the field lab finished gently scrubbing the pieces, they noticed faint carved lines. The fragments had been keyed, by means of numbered tags, to drawings made while the wood still lay in the house floor. These let the lab workers know immediately which part of the excavation the pieces had come from, and one of the girls went to the excavation to tell the students working in that square what she had found. Most of the board the pieces belonged to still lay buried, and no carving showed on what little of it had been washed free. It looked like an ordinary plank. Part of a wall lay on top of it, together with bits of rotten wood and midden that had been pushed into the house as the slide struck. This made it impossible to hose quickly and see the whole board or turn it over to look at the other side. The overlying material would first have to be documented and removed, and only then could the plank be moved. However, as an advance check, Daugherty decided to wash beneath the plank as it lay, clearing away enough of the mud to feel the undersurface for possible carving.

The idea worked. Reaching under just a little, his fingers touched grooves cut into the wood. Curiosity rose. What would this carving be? How large was the plank, and was it whole or broken? Days of work lay ahead before answers could be known. "It's a jigsaw puzzle," the log commented.

Two poles lashed together were sticking out of the mud on top of the carving, also a canoe paddle, a whale shoulder blade, and a broken roof plank. These were freed, photographed, drawn, lifted, and sent to the field lab. Beneath them was a box and a bundle of twigs of about finger thickness, probably to be twined into a sturdy burden basket or perhaps a fish trap. Then came two wooden wedges of the type used to split boards from cedar logs, a stone maul, and the skeleton of a puppy. Next was a wooden food dish about the size and shape of a serving platter today, a spear for catching salmon,

and part of a rake used for getting herring, which are small fish that swarm into shallow water in great numbers and are easily caught.

Seven days were spent carefully clearing the carved board. To raise it, crosspieces of wood were slipped underneath, others were laid on top, and the two sets were tied at the ends. The board was whole—and huge. It measured nearly seven meters long by one meter wide with only one apparent split running its length. Ten students took hold of the supports and lifted. Others stood alongside holding weak places. The prize was turned over, and for the first time the crew saw the carving—a whale. From what is known of early-day Indian houses along the Northwest Coast, Daugherty had expected to find interior decorations such as carved house posts and wall screens. The whale plank, as well as the earlier carved plank, bore this out.

Left: The large plank with a carving on its underside was removed from the excavation: *Below:* The carving of a whale is shown here emphasized with string.

VII
IN THE LAB

The whirring rotors of the helicopter set up such a wind that sand flew, and grass on the terrace above the beach blew flat. When the door slid open, Gleeson stepped forward to greet the arrivals with special eagerness. This was no ordinary flight. The helicopter was bringing the senior citizens from Neah Bay.

The calendar stood at August 26: Makah Day, the yearly celebration of the time when the tribe was officially presented with a United States flag and encouraged to exercise their rights as full citizens. This year of 1972 gave extra reasons to rejoice. The land at Ozette had been returned to tribal ownership after a long struggle. In the mid 1800's, the government

officials working out treaties with the Indians had set aside
an Ozette Reservation separate from the Makah Reservation.
So little was known about the people whose lives and lands
were being arranged that the negotiators failed to realize the
Ozettes were a Makah people, speaking the same language,
following the same traditions, and moving freely from one
village to another.

Later, when Ozette had to be abandoned to get the children
into school, new government officials came to believe there
no longer were any Ozette Indians, and they decided to
abolish the reservation. The Makahs protested, and finally
they had won. The land again was theirs. Traditions and
memories of the past had always been kept alive and now,
through the archaeological excavations, the tribe was getting
renewed, tangible evidence of their rich heritage.

The senior citizens had come to Ozette to see for themselves. The trail to the beach was too rough and long for
their aging legs, and they thought they'd never again see the
village site. Then Daugherty and one of his graduate students
arranged for the helicopter. Among the elders was a man
who lived at Ozette as a youth, and two of the women had
spent their girlhood summers in the village, going with their
families to fish during the months that school was not in
session. All of the group had relatives who were born at
Ozette or lived there.

The helicopter was giving them a chance to see this beach
again, to look out to the rocky island where sea lions climb
out of the water to rest, and beyond it to where migrating
whales spout. The elders could walk where they had played
and worked as children, and they could see the old house

The Marine helicopter lifted off from Ozette
carrying artifacts for the lab at Neah Bay.

where ancestors of their tribe had lived. Songs rose in their
hearts, for Makahs seem always to express deep feelings
through songs and dances. The women took drums from bags
carried on their arms and tapped them softly. Voices mingled
with the roar of distant waves on the reef, and feet danced
the old steps upon the earthen floor of the house. The thread
of tribal tradition seemed to stretch unbroken by the pass-
ing of the centuries.

The Makah Tribe has participated in the dig from the

beginning. They even fixed up a building in Neah Bay for the archaeologists to use as a laboratory and warehouse for the material from the excavation. It includes thousands of feet of shelves for storage, laboratory sinks and counters, preserving tanks, an apartment—everything needed to safeguard and analyze the Ozette discoveries. "The finest laboratory an archaeologist has ever had so close to his excavations," Daugherty calls it.

By the end of summer 1972 an incredible 13,000 artifacts had been flown from the site to the lab. They range from pieces as small as the wood shavings and plugs of sealskin floats up to roof supports and wall planks. The helicopter lands at the Ozette camp, loads up with artifacts and timbers and whalebones, then flies directly to the courtyard of the lab in Neah Bay.

Once recovered, the problem is to preserve the material, a process that is begun at the site. Artifacts and planks are cleaned, examined, and catalogued in the field lab, then set to soak in a special solution. In 1966 and 1967, glue diluted with water was used, but at that time there weren't any wooden artifacts to deal with, only bone (and stone, which didn't require treatment). Now there is wood and fiber to save, and new techniques are needed. Getting ideas on how to proceed is not easy because in all the world few archaeological sites have yielded wooden items in such concentration as at Ozette.

Walkways and walls from ancient villages in Britain have been found in bogs and remnants of lakeside habitations are known in Switzerland. Ships discovered in Scandinavia perhaps parallel Ozette preservation problems the most closely.

Some are from the Viking period, yet they are remarkably whole, with even chests and furnishings saved from decay by wet mud that sealed them for centuries. Scandinavian scientists have given advice on handling Ozette materials, and their suggestions have been adapted to fit the exact circumstances. Wood technologists at Washington State University and at the Forest Products Laboratory in Madison, Wisconsin, have also been consulted.

A basket may be light colored as it comes from the excavation, then darken in minutes on exposure to air, perhaps owing to oxidation, perhaps in reaction to light. If permitted to dry after so many centuries of being waterlogged, each cell within the fiber shrinks as it loses its moisture, and the whole piece turns brittle and falls apart. The only way to prevent such damage is to move each discovery quickly from the wet clay of the slide into the preserving solution of polyethylene glycol, commonly called Carbowax. This substance, distantly related to the antifreeze used in cars, comes as a pasty wax to be melted and mixed with water.

The usual treatment is to soak items in a 50 percent solution. However, some of the Ozette fishhooks, combs, and box fragments of hardwood didn't seem to respond well. In the hope that heat would help the preservative to penetrate the wood and speed the treatment period, the team tried gently cooking these pieces for an hour on several successive days, each time increasing the concentration of the Carbowax. The heat seemed to have no particular effect, however, and artifacts and planks now are simply soaked, some of them for months or even years. Different kinds of wood react differently, and new methods are constantly being worked out.

Left: At the Neah Bay laboratory, tanks filled with Carbowax receive the artifacts. They soak for weeks or even years.

Preservation occurs as the Carbowax
replaces water in the wood's cells.

As Carbowax soaks in, it replaces water in the wood's
cells with wax. This keeps the cells swollen and makes it possible for artifacts that would break otherwise to be safely
exposed to air. Of course, problems continue. One spindle
whorl persists in cracking. Seemingly the wax replaces the
water in its cells too rapidly, but cutting the strength of the
preservative solution has no effect. The whorl is carved from
hardwood, and it reacts differently from over 90 percent of
the artifacts, which are of softwood.

Another problem without answer so far is cherry bark. Indians used strips of it for wrapping handles and to bind harpoon ropes, because, like rawhide, cherry bark shrinks and tightens as it dries. But now that time has robbed the bark of its strength, the shrinking means trouble. The wrappings and bindings start to tear apart on drying, no matter how long they have been soaking. The only safe place to store them seems to be in the preservation tanks.

Bowls used for seal and whale oil pose a different sort of problem. Their cells are so saturated with oil that nothing Grosso tries seems to force wax into the wood. Soak the bowls for months, cook them in preservative, experiment with different percentages of chemicals—they still crack when taken from the tanks even for a few minutes. The only answer for now is to leave them soaking while thinking of something else to try. Maybe solvents such as alcohol and benzine can be used to draw the ancient oil out of the bowls so that the polyethylene can replace it. Or the decision may be to try a technique that has been used successfully in Scotland on waterlogged hardwood planks dating from the Roman period. This involves soaking the wood in a hydrochloric acid solution, then thoroughly washing it, and soaking it in acetone. After additional washing, it goes into Carbowax.

Several times containers have been brought to the lab with their original contents still inside. This calls for preserving two or more kinds of material at a time. An example is a woven wallet of cedar bark holding fishhooks with wooden shanks and bone points, a whetstone, extra pieces of bone, and a hank of thread. Another case is a whaler's basket holding lengths of cedar bark folded over mussel-shell harpoon heads to protect their edges. Daugherty and Grosso gingerly opened one of these pouches, brushing on hot water to saturate the bark and keep it from breaking. They found that the ends were split and woven to prevent fraying of the bark, and inside was an unbroken blade complete even to tiny wedges of wood still holding the barbs snug. The problem now is to preserve shell, bone, and fiber as a single piece, but in this instance Grosso doesn't expect difficulty. Shell and bone pose no problem, and the bark has responded well to treatment in polyethylene.

A cedar-bark pouch was carefully opened.

Raw materials often are found in the house, such as lumps of ochre for use as red paint, slabs of whale baleen for some purpose not yet understood, and twigs and roots tied into neat bundles ready for making into cords and baskets. These supplies, stored for future use, tell something of life at Ozette 500 years ago. So do hundreds of cedar splinters found lying on what once was the floor surface. They mark a part of the house where a woodworker must have been splitting boards or doing some carving—work that produces splinters by the score.

Inside the pouch was the head of a whale harpoon with its mussel-shell blade, bone barbs, and lashings still in place.

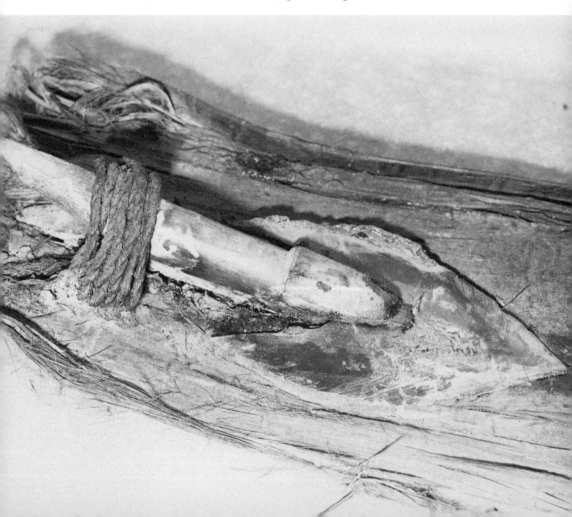

Above: Simple wooden utility boxes by the dozen were found in the house. *Right:* Jeff Mauger, project field foreman, demonstrates the old way of making such a box by steaming and bending a grooved board to form the sides.

To get a feeling of what woodworking must have been like at Ozette, one of the students duplicated wedges, mauls, and chisels from the old house, then used them to make squared boxes in the traditional way. In the old days these ranged in size from small boxes eight or ten centimeters across up to huge storage chests. Regardless of size, the four sides were made from a single board that was steamed and bent. The woodworker began by first splitting out a board and thinning it, then cutting vee-shaped grooves where the corners would come. The next step was to steam the board in wet seaweed laid over stones that had been heated in a fire. It then could be bent, forming three corners, and the side where the open ends met would later be closed with wooden pegs. A separate bottom piece would also be pegged on.

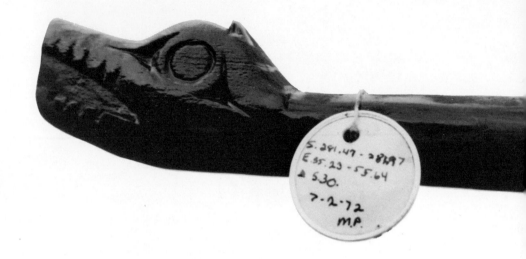

Two wolf heads decorating a long, thin stick *(above)*
and a club carved with an owl's head *(right)*
show the artistry of the early-day Ozettes.

The great variety of material filling the lab at Neah Bay
points to the intricacy of life at Ozette. These were not people
living in Spartan simplicity. On the contrary, they devised
every convenience their resources permitted, and they practiced a high level of artistry and ritual. Often the artwork
seems to be for its own sake, for its beauty rather than for any
utilitarian purpose. For example, a sleeping bench has rows
of round, flat shells painstakingly studded end on into the
wood, heavy-duty workbaskets have designs woven into them,
and a long stick used in weaving is carved with two wolf heads.
Sometimes the use or importance of an item cannot be known.
A heavy wooden club decorated with exquisitely carved owl
heads and a small carving of a man with a long thin nose
belong in this category. With this last piece not only is the
importance impossible to know, but determining what material it's carved from is proving difficult.

The long, thin face of the little man is carved in a style that seems to have been typical for centuries along much of the Northwest Coast.

The piece is about the size of a man's thumb and hollow on the inside. This suggests it might be a sea-lion's tooth or the tip of an antler, but the surface is so polished that the characteristic differences between the two substances no longer are apparent. X rays show nothing conclusive. The most promising way to tell would be to cut a thin slice off the bottom, prepare a slide, and examine it under a microscope. But this can be done only if it is possible to get a scraping somehow or a tiny core from the inside so as to avoid damage. The carving is small and fragile, its sides exceedingly thin.

Even when the intended purpose of artifacts such as the little man, and owl club stick can't be known, the simple fact that they existed so long ago has significance. It proves a rich life-style along the Northwest Coast at an earlier period than archaeologists have previously known much about. The Oz-ettes centuries ago developed a complicated technology to let them harvest the sea, and they also worked out a deep spiritual awareness of life and environment. Songs and dances and stories expressed this. So did artwork, whether as geometric design, realistic carvings of animals and faces, or mythical, symbolic portrayals.

Before the discoveries at Ozette, speculations about the role of art along the coast could only be based on artifacts collected by early-day Europeans and Americans, today scattered in museums as far distant as London and Leningrad. Now for the first time it is possible to study the contents of a single house that dates back to a time before Indian art in this region could have been influenced by contact from the outside. Previous thought tended to be that elaborate carving didn't develop until white traders made iron tools readily available, but the old house offers proof to the contrary.

Its artwork shows that remarkably fine carving was done at an early time using blades of shell, stone, and tooth such as those found in the excavations. Furthermore, in addition to these native materials, Northwest Coast Indians evidently

Metal must have been rare at Ozette in prehistoric times,
but a few woodworking tools with iron blades were found.

possessed iron before the earliest Europeans arrived along the
coast. Not much of it. Not enough for ordinary use. But
enough for a few special tools. Journals of several explorers
who arrived on the coast in the late 1700's mention that Indians instantly recognized the iron of ships' fittings and greatly
desired it. What little they already had they seemed to prize
above all else.

In the house, a dozen iron blades have been found. A few
are too broken to be sure what they once were like, but most
obviously were woodworking tools such as chisels and adzes.

Beaver teeth mounted in handles formed
an ancient but effective type of chisel.

The sharpness and durability of their edges must have been
regarded highly, but the supply of iron was so limited that few
men could hope to own such a blade. Most projects must have
been undertaken with other tools—very successfully. For instance, the lines carved into the whale screen are the exact
width of the beaver-tooth chisels found in the house. The
same is true of the plank fancifully carved with the birds and
canines.

As yet, the source of the Ozette iron is not known. The
only tests run so far show a high carbon content. Perhaps

Some of the iron blades had nearly rusted away;
others had been almost perfectly preserved.

further testing will reveal enough distinctions to permit check-
ing against the known characteristics of iron from various locations. No mines are located in the Northwest, although the
iron could have come from mines in the East. Such a valuable
material would have been worth trading across the continent,
the way pipestone from Minnesota is known to have reached
the Pacific Northwest in prehistoric times. Or the iron could
have been traded across the Bering Strait from Siberia and
then made its way down the coast from tribe to tribe.

Another possibility might be Oriental junks. Chinese records mention a voyage of exploration to America more than
one thousand years ago. Also, the ocean current flows across
the Pacific from the Japanese coast to the Olympic coast.
Several disabled fishing vessels have drifted across within historic time, and there are indications of others in earlier times.
Even today net floats used by Japanese fishermen wash ashore
on the beaches of Washington and British Columbia. Ship-
wrecks or ships coming deliberately seem a probable source
of the iron, and some such contact is further borne out by a

brass tack about a centimeter long found just below the floor level of the old house. Daugherty speculates that brass would not have been traded far in the form of a tack, which would be neither utilitarian nor decorative. Such an item, as it was passed from tribe to tribe, most likely would have been altered, and this tack shows no such indication. Consequently, it seems probable that it reached the Olympic coast as part of some sort of drift from across the Pacific, perhaps a wrecked ship. Much more evidence is needed before any details can be reasoned out.

A different sort of prize has been the discovery of three complete looms and parts of others in the house. Previously, weaving has been credited to tribes living farther inland, around Puget Sound, but not to those along the outer coast. There is no early mention of looms on the ocean coast and so their presence was doubted, but Ozette gives proof to the contrary.

Mountain goats are known to have furnished wool for Northwest Coast people, and special dogs were kept by some tribes for their poodlelike fleece. At Ozette the dogs alone must have provided the main source of wool because mountain goats are not native in the Olympic Mountains. Gustafson identified more than 200 dog bones from the early trench. They are from two sizes of animals, with the smaller belonging to a type unknown today, probably the wool dogs. The journals of early explorers tell of such dogs being kept on islands to prevent their breeding with camp dogs and possibly lessening the wooliness of future generations. Fluff from fireweed seedheads and cattails sometimes was mixed in with the wool, as in the case of the plaid blanket. One of the Makah high-school girls helping to excavate set up a loom like those

A Makah crew member experimented with a
replica of one of the looms from the old house.

found in the house and, using ordinary yarn, wove a sample
fabric in the old way.

Several of the artifacts filling the shelves at the lab give a
special feeling for the life of the people who made them and
used them. There is a cooking box that must have had one
too many hot rocks dropped into it, for a hole is burned
through the bottom and has been patched with a small piece

The bottom of a box had been burned through, then patched.

of wood laced on to cover it. There is also a small-sized bow-
and-arrow set that must have belonged to a young boy, and
several paddles like those used in Ping-Pong. The paddles
were a puzzle until some of the Makah elders explained them.
As children they played with some identical to these from the
old house, hitting shuttlecocks made from lengths of thimble-
berry stem and fitted with feathers. Another item that gives a

Paddles were used in a shuttlecock game.

sense of contact with the past is a harpoon shaft with sea-otter teeth embedded in it to provide a firm handgrip for the man whose place it was to stand in the bow of the canoe and hurl the harpoon into the whale.

Perhaps the find that puzzles Daugherty the most is a row of whalebones lined up just outside the south wall of the house. Two skulls rest beside each other facing south, and next to them are several vertebrae and part of a jawbone. Whalebones are huge and heavy and carrying them up from the beach would have been hard work that probably wasn't a necessary part of butchering and dividing the blubber and meat. Maybe the bones served as a trophy to proclaim the

Right: Whalebones lined up outside the old house.

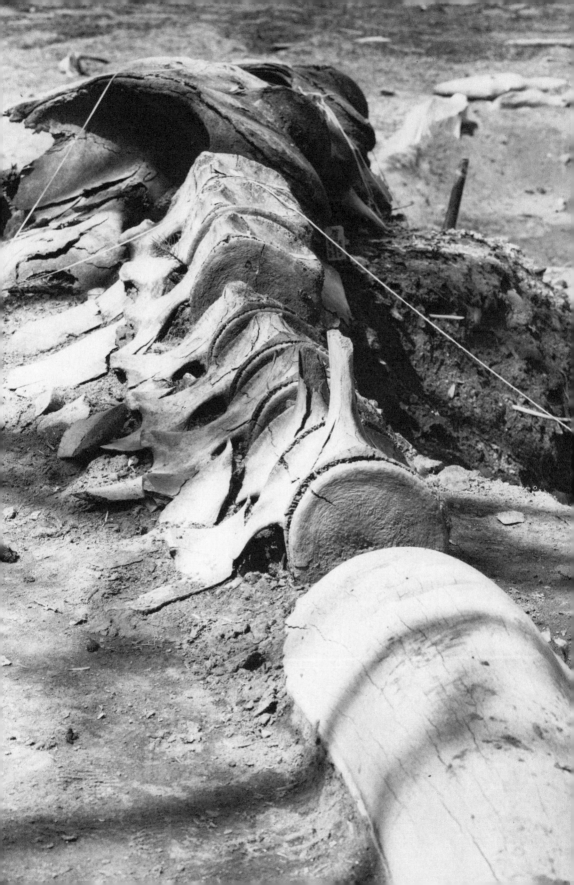

house as belonging to a whale hunter. Or perhaps they were somehow a part of the ritualism that went with whaling. No written mention of anything like this arrangement is known. None of the Makahs alive today can explain it. Further excavation and study may give a clue, or it may be that the meaning never will be understood.

The archaeologists and the Makahs are now planning an expansion of the laboratory in Neah Bay. Material from the one house has filled the existing shelves, and added space is needed for preservation work and study as well as for storage. Seven thousand more artifacts were recovered during 1972, bringing the total to 20,000 by the close of the 1973 field school. In size they range from haircombs to house planks. One of the graduate students working on her Ph.D. is identifying the various kinds of wood, an immensely important study since woodworking is considered the outstanding cultural feature of Northwest Coast Indians. No other groups in native America rivaled them in the use of wood, both for utility and for art; yet until the Ozette discoveries no archaeologist ever has been able to see the full range of items that equipped a household in the days before white men arrived.

For example, it long has been known that western red cedar was used for house planks and canoes and that cedar bark was stripped from the trees to weave into mats and baskets. Cedar is a wood that splits easily, and this simplified working with limited tools such as a chisel and adze. The bark peels from the trunks in strips twenty feet long. It splits readily, too, and is wonderfully pliable for weaving. But for all its importance, the use of cedar actually was only a part of the Indians' knowledge of wood technology, according to the evidence that the old house is making available. Many kinds of wood were used for containers, tools, and weapons—in fact, practically all the kinds of wood that were available, including some that would not be expected, such as crab apple and twinberry, and also wood from kinds of trees that don't grow conveniently close to Ozette.

Microscopic examination of cell structure permits identification. Bowls tend to be made of red alder or Oregon ash, woods that carve easily and have no odor or strong taste of

Jan Friedman identified the woods used in the various artifacts.

their own that would affect the flavor of oil or food. Bows need to be of a wood that bends well and is strong, and those from the house indicate that big-leaf maple and Pacific yew were the preferred choices. Wedges must be able to resist pounding, and it has always been supposed they were made of yew because of its known strength. However, most of those in the house are of Sitka spruce.

Another specialized study of materials from Ozette is being made by a graduate student working on baskets, cordage,

Ozette crew members practiced basketmaking techniques.

clothing, and mats for his Ph.D. He analyzes both what the items are made from and also the techniques of weaving them. He takes basketry lessons from Makah women in order to better understand the whole process and is teaching others of the crew to weave too. When one's own fingers have twined weft and warp and produced a basket, the whole process of uncovering one made centuries ago takes on added meaning.

The various studies often bring Makahs to the lab to see what is going on, and they also come when they hear the

Makah senior citizens helped identify the artifacts.

helicopter arriving from the site with new discoveries. Sometimes even if the elders haven't themselves used objects similar to those from the house, they can recognize them and help with identification because they have heard their parents or grandparents tell of them. Makahs always have kept their culture alive, and the elders deeply enjoy this tie to their past. The Ozette project is like a window onto the richness and variety of their ancestors' life. It both stirs memories and also gives young people a clear look at things they previously had heard about but not seen. Woodworking classes at the high school find heightened interest in carving traditional motifs such as Killer Whale, Raven, and Eagle. Basketmaking lessons and Makah language lessons, given daily by village women, are taking on added meaning as students see the physical evidence of their heritage that is coming from the old house.

Tribal members also are working with an archaeologist from the Ozette Project in surveying for sites on all of the land that belonged to the Makahs in prehistoric time. One village seems to have been situated for deer and elk hunting, as well as sea mammal hunting, to judge from the animal bones and types of artifacts found, and another evidently was primarily for fishing and harvesting shellfish from a reef. At a third, which is on an island, the crew expected to find mostly fishing equipment, because even after the coming of white men the site was favored among Makahs and nearby tribes for its excellent halibut fishing. However, test excavations so far have revealed an unexpected abundance of seal bones but little evidence of halibut. There are dozens of sites to check.

At Ozette, Daugherty and Gleeson had expected to finish excavating the old house during the 1973 field school, but

Left, top: Classes at Neah Bay High School keep alive the ancient tradition of wood carving. *Bottom:* Many of the basketry techniques used today are the same as those represented in the old house.

One of the Makahs on the crew used an auger to sample shell midden for Ed Friedman, leader of the survey.

by summer's end it still was not quite done. Investigating the one house has taken three and one-half years and cost more money than any other single archaeological study in the United States. Knowledge gained from it will continue to grow even after work on the deposits themselves is finally complete. The specialized studies will be finished, and Daugherty at last can begin analysis of the full inventory of the house contents.

Also, he knows where five other houses lie buried and expects to excavate two of them. The other three he will leave untouched. New techniques may well be developed in the future that will permit better methods of investigation or of preservation. Besides, Daugherty feels that it is best for someone else eventually to direct work on the buried houses at Ozette. That way new knowledge and a different personal background will be brought to the study. A separate expert opinion, also based on prolonged field excavation, will be added to his own. Leaving the three houses buried is like having a savings account at the bank.

The two additional houses Daugherty will excavate stand

A hoist lifted the crew from a Coast Guard boat
to the top of Tatoosh Island for a site survey.

Panoramic view of Ozette site. Excavation trench
can be seen at left center, camp to the right.

higher on the hillside than the one now practically finished.
In fact, parts of them were knocked into the old house when
the slide struck. An elaborate box carved with a bird's face
and using fish or shark teeth to outline the design and molars
from a sea otter as eyes came from one of these other houses.
So did the carved whale fin inlaid with teeth. These artifacts
lay in the slide material that covered the excavated house and
it is this position, above the floor level, that indicates they
belonged to the upper houses. Evidently they were swept

along by the mud as it smashed those houses and carried parts
of them downslope.

Perhaps the houses still to be excavated hold ceremonial
gear of a kind not present in the first house, which quite possibly was lived in only seasonally. Termite damage to the
walls and extensive repairs suggest that it was old and in
poor condition. Maybe the upper houses will prove in better
condition or more finely constructed. Maybe they will be even
larger. Their posts may be carved. Dance masks and equip-

Among the items to be exhibited in the new museum are an ornate box front *(above)* and a carved whalebone club *(right)*.

ment used by medicine men may be present. There is no way to tell now, but excavation will bring answers. It will take another three years—or four or five or six—to study these houses as carefully as the team has studied the first one.

A wealth of additional artifacts is certain, and the Makahs plan to build a museum in Neah Bay to display them and to provide study space for analyzing them. The combs and shell necklaces, the boxes, bowls, and chisels, the whaling gear and canoe paddles—everything—will remain with the tribe whose

ancestors made them and used them. Nothing is to be taken away. Already Daugherty and Harvey Rice have gone to Washington, D.C., with Joseph Lawrence, the new Tribal Chairman, to testify before a Congressional committee considering a grant for the museum. A prime goal of archaeology is to give man a knowledge of his past so that he can better understand the present and plan for the future. Results from Ozette fulfill this aim, and the Makah museum will both safeguard the physical discoveries and present the knowledge that has been gained.

The museum is part of a long effort by the tribe and the archaeologists. The search for the past at Ozette began twenty-six years ago when Daugherty first surveyed the site, and it will go on for several years more. The ancient houses still to be uncovered promise an even greater understanding of the long relationship between man and environment on the Northwest Coast.

INDEX

indicates illustrations

A native of Washington's Olympic Peninsula, Richard D. Daugherty, Ph.D., is a professor of anthropology at Washington State University and director of the Washington Archaeological Research Center. He has excavated in Africa and Europe but is best known for his work in the prehistory of the Pacific Northwest. Through appointment by President Lyndon B. Johnson he has served on the nation's Advisory Council on Historic Preservation and, in his own state, has been given special commendation by the legislature for his work there. In 1973, the governor of Washington made a unique joint award to Dr. Daugherty and the Makah Indian tribe honoring their effort in recovering and preserving prehistoric art at the Ozette Indian site.

Ruth Kirk, a journalist who specializes in natural history, lived on the Olympic Peninsula and met Dr. Daugherty there in 1966 as the Ozette excavations were beginning. She has followed the work closely ever since, both in the field and in the laboratory. Like Dr. Daugherty, she has many friends in the Indian villages along the Olympic coast, and this friendship enhances the material presented in *Hunters of the Whale*.

Mrs. Kirk and her husband, Louis, live in Tacoma, where he produces features for educational television.